Pies & Tarts

GENERAL EDITOR
CHUCK WILLIAMS

RECIPES
JOHN PHILLIP CARROLL

PHOTOGRAPHY
ALLAN ROSENBERG

TIME
LIFE
BOOKS

Time-Life Books
is a division of TIME LIFE INC.,
a wholly owned subsidary of
THE TIME INC. BOOK COMPANY

President: John M. Fahey

TIME-LIFE BOOKS
President: Mary Davis
Publisher: Robert H. Smith
Vice President and Associate Publisher:
  Trevor Lunn
Vice President and Associate Publisher:
  Susan J. Maruyama
Director of Special Markets: Frances C. Mangan
Marketing Director: Regina Hall
Editorial Director: Donia Ann Steele

WILLIAMS-SONOMA
Founder/Vice-Chairman: Chuck Williams

WELDON OWEN INC.
President: John Owen
Publisher: Wendely Harvey
Senior Editor: Laurie Wertz
Consulting Editor: Norman Kolpas
Copy Editor: Sharon Silva
Design: John Bull, The Book Design Company
Production: Stephanie Sherman, Mick Bagnato
Food Photographer: Allan Rosenberg
Associate Food Photographer: Allen V. Lott
Primary Food & Prop Stylist: Sandra Griswold
Food Stylist: Heidi Gintner
Prop Assistant: Karen Nicks
Glossary Illustrations: Alice Harth

The Williams-Sonoma Kitchen Library
conceived and produced by Weldon Owen Inc.
814 Montgomery St., San Francisco, CA 94133

In collaboration with Williams-Sonoma
100 North Point, San Francisco, CA 94133

Production by Mandarin Offset, Hong Kong
Printed in Hong Kong

A Weldon Owen Production

Library of Congress
Cataloging-in-Publication Data:

Carroll, John Phillip.
    Pies & tarts / general editor, Chuck
Williams ; recipes, John Phillip Carroll ;
photography, Allan Rosenberg.
        p.   cm. — (Williams-Sonoma kitchen
    library)
    Includes index.
    ISBN 0-7835-0200-1
    1. Pies. I. Williams, Chuck. II. Title.
III. Title: Pies and tarts. IV. Series.
TX773.C344   1992
641.8'652—dc20   92-10315
                                   CIP

Contents

BASIC RECIPES 12

SUMMER PIES & TARTS 19

WINTER PIES & TARTS 47

PIES & TARTS FOR ALL SEASONS 75

INTRODUCTION

Easy as pie. No phrase better describes a task that is simplicity itself.
How ironic it is, then, that most home cooks regard the art of making pies
and tarts as anything but easy.

This book aims to dispel the fear and uncertainty from pie making.
Its premise is that anyone who wants to, regardless of his or her cooking skill or
experience, can make a delicious and attractive pie or tart with unparalleled ease.

On the following pages, you'll find all the information you need to make
any pie or tart—from selecting a few pieces of basic equipment, to making
doughs and crusts, to shaping, filling and baking. Throughout we've made the
instructions exceptionally simple and reassuring.

These fundamentals are followed by 43 delicious, easy-to-prepare recipes,
organized into three chapters: those featuring fresh peak-of-season fruit, robust
winter pies and tarts, and classic recipes to be served year-round. Each is accom-
panied by a full-page photograph to guide and inspire you in its preparation.

If you've never made a pie or tart before, please let me offer one final
word of advice: Try it *now,* without hesitation, and see just how easy it really
can be. Don't let anything stop you. If you don't have a pie or tart pan, use a
shallow baking dish. If you're daunted by making the dough, buy a good
commercial refrigerated (not frozen) dough from the supermarket. Don't even
labor or fuss over trimming the dough to make it look perfect; a rustic
pie can be beautiful, too. In fact, you don't even need dough to make
a pie. Just fill a baking dish with fruit filling
and sprinkle on a crumb topping.

When that first effort comes out of
the oven, its filling bubbling and its crust
crisp and golden, I'm sure you'll agree that
there *is* delectable truth in the words
"easy as pie."

Chuck Williams

EQUIPMENT

From pastry wheels to rolling pins, pie pans to cooling racks,
simple, good-quality tools make the job easier.

All you really need to bake a pie or a tart is an oven and some sort of baking dish. But a few pieces of relatively inexpensive equipment will help you work more efficiently for consistently excellent results.

Pie pans and tart rings, measuring 9 inches (23 cm) in diameter within their rims and holding approximately 4½ cups (36 fl oz/1.1 l), accommodate most standard recipes. Those made of metal, preferably aluminum, conduct heat best, producing crisper crusts; ovenproof glass and porcelain pie pans also work well and are attractive for table service.

It is not essential that your equipment exactly match the items shown here. The most important guideline to follow is to choose the best-quality, most functional tools available. Over the long run, well-made kitchen equipment will save you money, providing years of reliable use.

1. Porcelain Pie Dish
For fruit pies without bottom crusts. Because porcelain conducts heat less effectively than metal or glass, it prevents fillings from scorching. Choose a dish about 2 inches (5 cm) deep.

2. Cooling Rack
Allows air to circulate under a baked pie while it cools in its pan, ensuring that the bottom crust stays crisp.

3. Kitchen Scissors
For neatly trimming dough around the edges of a pie pan.

4. Dowel-Type Rolling Pin
For best control when rolling out dough. Select a sturdy hardwood pin, at least 12 inches (30 cm) long. To prevent warping, do not wash; wipe clean with a dry cloth.

5. Pastry Wheel
Cuts lattice dough strips with plain edges.

6. Fluted Pastry Wheel
Cuts lattice dough strips with decorative, or crinkled, edges.

7. Wire Whisk
Essential for blending custard fillings and beating egg whites. Use a smaller, less open whisk, 10–12 inches (25–30 cm) long, for custards, and a balloon type for whipping egg whites.

8. Dough Scraper
Useful for lifting pie dough and for cleaning work surfaces after dough is made. Choose a sturdy stainless-steel scraper with metal or wooden handle.

9. Pastry Blender
For cutting butter or shortening (lard) into flour when making pastry dough by hand.

10. Rolling Pin with Handles
The most commonly used rolling pin for pie dough. Choose one with ball-bearing handles for smooth rolling, and a hardwood surface at least 12 inches (30 cm) long. To prevent warping, do not wash; wipe clean with a dry cloth.

11. Pie Server
For cutting and serving pie. Choose one with a sturdy, stainless-steel, wedge-shaped blade.

12. Tart Pan
Removable bottom of standard 9-inch (23-cm) pan allows tart to be unmolded. Fluted sides give pastry crust a sturdy and attractive edge.

13. Metal Pie Pan
Metal—preferably aluminum—conducts heat best for a crisp, browned crust. Standard size is 9 inches (23 cm), measured inside the rim. If using black steel or dark anodized aluminum, which absorbs heat faster, reduce oven temperature by 25°F (15°C).

14. Glass Pie Dish
Attractive container for baking and serving pie. Holds heat well for crisp, brown crusts—although baking temperature should be increased by 25°F (15°C). Choose good-quality ovenproof glass.

15. Pastry Brush
For brushing glazes onto crust. Choose one with fairly flexible, not-too-thick, natural bristles.

16. Tart Ring
Allows easy transfer of tart to serving plate. Made of tinned steel, may be rectangular, square or round. Must be used on top of a baking sheet.

17. Baking Sheet
Provides a flat surface for tart rings or free-form tarts. Select heavy aluminum or tinned steel.

MAKING A PIE

Although diverse in flavor and appearance,
both pies and tarts are easy to make and follow the
same basic procedures.

The how-to photographs shown here illustrate the
most basic steps in shaping and decorating crusts.
Follow them carefully, and you will quickly master
the techniques. The various pie and tart pastries
(see recipes, pages 12–16) can all be mixed by hand,
and this is certainly the best way to become familiar
with pastry making. A food processor does a fine job
too, although you must be careful not to overmix
the dough.

   Pastry is rolled out on a lightly floured surface,
which may be wood, marble or even a flat countertop.
Some crusts, however, require no rolling at all. Crumb
crusts (step 9), for example, are simply patted into the
pan, and both the rich tart pastry (recipe on page 14)
and the chocolate-walnut pastry (recipe on page 16)
may be pressed and patted into the pan using your
fingertips as well. Once the pastry is in the pan, it
may, depending upon the recipe, require partial or
full baking (step 8) before it is filled.

   Double-crust pies may be attractively finished
on top in a number of ways. Pastry may be cut
into strips and woven into a lattice (page 10) that
shows off fruit fillings. Or dough scraps and
trimmings may be cut with a sharp knife or small
pastry cutters into leaves or other shapes, then
moistened with water and placed on the top crust
in a decorative pattern.

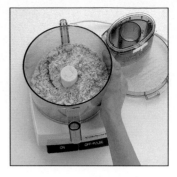

1. *Mixing pastry.*
To mix by hand, toss together
flour and other dry ingredients
in bowl. Blend in shortening or
butter, pressing down with
pastry blender, until mixture
resembles coarse crumbs.

2. *Using a food processor.*
Alternatively, add fat (butter is
used here) to dry ingredients in
processor with steel blade,
pulsing machine until mixture
resembles coarse flakes and
crumbs.

3. Adding liquid.
A little at a time, add liquid, pulsing machine—or stirring ingredients in bowl with fork—after each addition. Continue adding liquid just until pastry forms rough, damp mass.

4. Patting pastry together.
With floured hands and working on lightly floured surface, pat pastry together to form round, smooth cake; for double-crust pies, make 2 cakes, one slightly larger than the other.

5. Rolling out pastry.
Pastry can be used now, or wrapped in plastic wrap and refrigerated for up to 2 days. On floured surface, roll out into circle about 2 inches (5 cm) larger than the diameter of pie or tart pan.

6. Lining pan.
Transfer pastry to pan, patting it in to fit pan's shape. On tart pan, fold in overhanging dough to make sides thicker. On pie pan, trim dough with scissors, leaving 1 inch (2.5 cm) of overhang.

7. Fluting pastry.
For single-crust pie, decoratively flute pastry around rim. Here, a thumb is pressed into pastry at regular intervals (see glossary, page 106, for other techniques). For double-crust pies, flute once top crust is in place, to seal edges together.

8. Prebaking.
For partially or fully baked crust, line pastry with double thickness of foil in which a few holes have been poked. Bake 8 minutes at 425°F (220°C); remove foil and bake 4 minutes more for partially baked crust, 8–10 minutes for fully baked.

9. Forming crumb crust.
Combine crumbs and other ingredients following recipe instructions. With fingertips, pat and press crumbs into pan to cover bottom and sides evenly, taking care not to make sides too thick.

9

LATTICE TOP

A lattice top is made by weaving pastry strips directly on a filled pie. It's a nice way to show off fruit fillings—especially berries and peaches.

1. After rolling out pastry for top crust, cut it into 12 strips each about ¾ inch (2 cm) wide. Strips will be of varying lengths. Use longer strips near center of pie and shorter ones near edges. Cross two longest strips over center of filled pie. Place second long strip over top cross strip.

2. Now make lattice top as shown: Fold back every other strip and lay cross strip in place, then return folded-back strips to their original position. Continue weaving in this fashion, working from center of pie toward edges, until all strips are used.

3. When all strips are in place, trim off any overhanging pastry with scissors. Brush edges of pastry lightly with water and press gently on strips all around to seal them to bottom crust. Finally, flute around rim with your thumb.

PIE SHELLS AND SINGLE-CRUST PIES

Single-crust, or open-face, pies have no top crust. The bottom crust, called a pie shell, can be filled unbaked, partially baked or fully baked, depending upon the recipe.

UNBAKED PIE SHELLS

There should be about 1 inch (2.5 cm) of pastry hanging over the side of the pan. Fold it under to make an upstanding rim around the edge of the pan, then flute the edge with your fingertips. It is now ready to be filled and baked according to the recipe.

PARTIALLY BAKED AND FULLY BAKED PIE SHELLS

For a partially baked pie shell, prick the bottom and sides of the shell all over with the tines of a fork. So the dough will keep its shape, form a double-thick 12-inch (30-cm) square of aluminum foil, poke a few holes in it, then press it snugly into the pastry-lined pan. Bake in a preheated 425°F (220°C) oven for 8 minutes. Lift out the foil and continue baking about 4 minutes longer, or until the pastry looks dry but not brown. If it puffs up while baking, poke it gently with a fork. Remove from the oven and set on a rack. Cool completely.

For a fully baked pie shell, proceed as directed for a partially baked shell, but after removing the foil bake for 8–10 minutes more, or until the pastry is light brown, crisp and dry. Let cool completely on a rack before filling.

DOUBLE-CRUST PIES

After filling the pie as directed in the recipe, brush the rim of the bottom crust with water. Lay the rolled-out top crust over the pie and trim the pastry all around so you have about ½ inch (12 mm) of overhang. Press firmly around the rim to seal the crusts together, then fold the overhang under itself all around to make an upstanding edge. Flute the edge. With a small knife, cut 4 or 5 slits, or vents, in the top crust so steam can escape during baking. Double-crust pies are usually baked at a high temperature for about 20 minutes, to cook the pastry, then the heat is reduced for the remainder of baking.

Fruit pies sometimes boil over during baking. To ensure a clean oven, place a large sheet of aluminum foil on the rack underneath the pie.

If during baking the edges of the crust brown too much, remove the pie from the oven and carefully cover the edges with strips of aluminum foil, molding them to fit the pie, then continue baking.

Clockwise from top right: Double crust, single crust, crumb crust, lattice top

Basic Pie Pastry

Crisp and flaky, a good crust for custard, chiffon and fresh-fruit pies. For successful pastry making, follow these three rules: take care not to overblend the fat and flour, add sufficient water so that the dough can be rolled out easily (better a bit too much water than not enough), and handle the pastry no more than necessary. Overblending, too little water and too much handling can make a crust tough. If you like the taste of butter, use it in place of shortening, or try a mixture of butter and shortening. The crust will be firmer than that made with shortening only.

FOR A 9-INCH (23-CM) PIE SHELL:

1½ cups (6 oz/185 g) all-purpose (plain) flour
½ teaspoon salt
½ cup (4 oz/125 g) vegetable shortening
   (vegetable lard)
3–4 tablespoons cold water, more or less

FOR A 9-INCH (23-CM) DOUBLE-CRUST PIE:

2¼ cups (9 oz/280 g) all-purpose (plain) flour
¾ teaspoon salt
¾ cup (6 oz/180 g) vegetable shortening
   (vegetable lard)
6–7 tablespoons cold water, more or less

*H*AND METHOD: Combine the flour and salt in a mixing bowl and toss together. Drop in the shortening. With your fingertips, two knives or a pastry blender, blend the ingredients together, working quickly, until you have a mixture of tiny, irregular flakes and bits about the size of coarse bread crumbs. Sprinkle on the water 1 tablespoon at a time, stirring gently with a fork after each addition. Add just enough water for the dough to form a rough mass.

With floured hands pat the dough into a smooth cake—or into 2 cakes, one just slightly larger than the other, if you are making a double-crust pie. The dough is now ready to use. It is not necessary to chill this dough, although for convenience it may be wrapped in plastic wrap and refrigerated for up to 2 days.

FOOD PROCESSOR METHOD: Because the food processor works so fast, it is very easy to overblend basic pastry, which results in a tough crust. Follow these instructions carefully, and you should be trouble-free. With the steel blade attached, place the flour, salt and shortening (in one lump) in the work bowl. Process with 15 rapid off-on pulses; the mixture should look light and dry and will resemble tiny, irregular flakes and crumbs. Add 2 tablespoons water (4 tablespoons if you are making a double-crust pie) and process again in 5 rapid off-on pulses. Add 1 more tablespoon water (2 tablespoons for a double-crust pie) and process in 3 rapid pulses. Stop and feel the dough (taking care not to touch the blade); it should be just damp enough to mass together. If necessary, add more water by teaspoonfuls, processing for just an instant after each addition. The total mixing time is less than 1 minute, and the dough should not form a ball; it should remain a rough, shaggy mass. Use it right away or chill it, as described in the hand method (above).

ROLLING OUT THE DOUGH: Roll the dough out on a floured surface (using the larger piece if it is the bottom of a double-crust pie) until it is about ⅛ inch (3 mm) thick and 12 inches (30 cm) in diameter, or about 2 inches (5 cm) larger than the top of the pie pan. Try to keep the dough as round as possible.

Transfer the rolled-out pastry to the pie pan. Pat the pastry in around the edges to fit the pan's shape. If you are making a double-crust pie, roll out the remaining pastry for the top crust and set it aside on waxed paper.

Tart Pastry

Because it is made with butter and has a higher proportion of fat than a basic pie pastry, tart pastry is firm and crumbly rather than flaky. Use this recipe whenever you want the taste of butter to come through. It may be made in a food processor or by hand.

1¼ cups (5 oz/155 g) all-purpose (plain) flour
1 tablespoon sugar
¼ teaspoon salt
½ cup (4 oz/125 g) unsalted butter, chilled
2 tablespoons, or more, cold water

FOOD PROCESSOR METHOD: Place the flour, sugar and salt in the work bowl of a processor. Cut the butter into tablespoon-sized pieces and add them. Process, using rapid off-on pulses, until the mixture resembles small particles about the size of oatmeal flakes. Add 1 tablespoon of the water and process a couple of seconds. Add another tablespoon of the water and process

with 3 or 4 off-on pulses. Feel the dough; it should be damp enough to form a rough mass. Add a few more drops of water if necessary to achieve the correct consistency.

Dump the dough onto a work surface, gather it together and pat it into a cake. The dough may be used right away, although you may find that it is easier to roll out if it is wrapped in plastic wrap and chilled for 30 minutes or so, especially if the day is very hot.

HAND METHOD: Combine the flour, sugar and salt in a mixing bowl and toss together. Cut the butter into bits and drop them into the bowl. With your fingertips, two knives or a pastry blender, blend the ingredients together until the mixture resembles small particles about the size of oatmeal flakes. Sprinkle 1 tablespoon water over the flour mixture, then stir gently with a fork. Sprinkle on another tablespoon of water and stir it in as well. Feel the dough; it should be damp enough to form a rough mass, but not wet. Add a few more drops of water if necessary to achieve the correct consistency. Dump the dough onto a work surface, gather it together and pat it into a cake. Use it right away or chill it, as described in the food processor method (above).

Roll the dough out on a generously floured work surface until it is about ⅛ inch (3 mm) thick and 11 inches (28 cm) in diameter, or about 2 inches (5 cm) larger than the top of a 9-inch (23-cm) tart pan. Try to keep the shape as round as possible.

Transfer the rolled-out pastry to the tart pan. Pat some of the overhang back in around the edge to make the sides of the tart shell a little thicker than the bottom. Trim off any remaining overhang. The tart shell may now be filled unbaked, partially baked or fully baked, depending upon the recipe (see page 10 for detailed instructions on prebaking).

Makes one 9-inch (23-cm) tart shell

13

Rich Tart Pastry

Sweeter and richer than the preceding recipe for tart pastry, with a sandy, cookielike texture similar to shortbread. Although this dough can be rolled out, it is easily pressed into a tart pan with your fingers—a boon if you don't like to roll out pastry. This buttery crust is a good foundation for fresh-fruit fillings.

1¼ cups (5 oz/155 g) all-purpose (plain) flour
¼ teaspoon salt
3 tablespoons (1½ oz/45 g) sugar
10 tablespoons (5 oz/155 g) unsalted butter, chilled
1 egg yolk
1½ tablespoons, or more, cold water

FOOD PROCESSOR METHOD: Place the flour, salt and sugar in the work bowl of a processor. Cut the butter into tablespoon-sized pieces and add them. Process, using rapid off-on pulses, until the mixture resembles small particles about the size of oatmeal flakes. In a small bowl, stir together the egg yolk and 1½ tablespoons water. With the processor running, pour the egg mixture into the bowl. Stop the processor and feel the dough; it should be damp enough to form a rough mass. If it is too dry, add a few more drops of water. Dump the dough onto a work surface and gather it into a ball.

HAND METHOD: Combine the flour, salt and sugar in a mixing bowl and toss together. Cut the butter into bits and drop them into the bowl. With your fingertips, two knives or a pastry blender, blend the ingredients together until the mixture resembles small particles about the size of oatmeal flakes. In a small bowl, stir together the egg yolk and 1½ tablespoons water. Add the egg mixture to the flour mixture and stir gently with a fork until the egg mixture is evenly distributed. Feel the dough; it should be damp enough to form a rough mass. If it is

too dry, add a few more drops of water. Dump the dough onto a work surface and gather it into a ball.

With your fingers press and pat walnut-sized pieces of dough over the bottom and sides of a 9-inch (23-cm) tart pan, leaving no gaps and making it as even as you can. (If you wish to roll the dough out, wrap it well in plastic wrap and chill for about 1 hour. Then roll it out on a generously floured work surface.) The tart shell may now be filled unbaked, partially baked or fully baked, depending upon the recipe (see page 10 for detailed instructions on prebaking).

Makes one 9-inch (23-cm) tart shell

Crumb Crust

Make crumbs in a food processor or crush them with a rolling pin, using graham crackers, gingersnaps, biscotti or chocolate wafers (if using chocolate wafers, use 2 cups (7 oz/220 g) crumbs). Whatever your choice, be sure it is fresh; the taste of stale crackers and cookies will haunt your pie. Although not essential, briefly baking a crumb crust before filling it will make it a little crisper.

1½ cups (5 oz/165 g) crumbs (*see note, above*)
2 tablespoons sugar
pinch of salt
½ cup (4 oz/125 g) unsalted butter, melted

Combine the crumbs, sugar and salt in a mixing bowl and toss together. Add the butter and stir vigorously until blended.

With your fingers press and pat the mixture over the bottom and sides of a 9-inch (23-cm) pie pan, taking care not to make the sides too thick.

If you wish, bake the crust in a preheated 325°F (165°C) oven for 8 minutes, then cool completely before filling.

Makes one 9-inch (23-cm) pie shell

Meringue Topping

Here is a good meringue that remains light and tender without shrinking and weeping. It makes enough to cover a 9-inch (23-cm) pie with a thick layer. If you prefer a thin meringue, halve the ingredients. It may also be piped on through a pastry bag, in a decorative border or crosshatch pattern if you wish.

A caution on eggs: In recent years, there has been increased concern about the threat of contracting salmonellosis (a food-borne illness caused by salmonella bacteria) from raw or lightly cooked eggs. Some recipes in this book, including meringue, are made with the latter. The amount of risk is very slight, but it should be noted that those who are elderly, very young or immunocompromised will be the most seriously affected if stricken with food poisoning. An egg mixture that is heated to 165°F (75°C) is safe. Also, be sure to refrigerate any pie with a milk- or egg-based filling or a cream or meringue topping.

⅔ cup (5 fl oz/160 ml) egg whites (about 5)
½ cup (4 oz/125 g) sugar
½ teaspoon cream of tartar
¼ teaspoon salt

Preheat a broiler (griller). Combine the egg whites and sugar in a large mixing bowl and set the bowl in a pan of simmering water. Stir gently for a minute or so, until the sugar has dissolved and the mixture is warm. Remove the bowl from the water and add the cream of tartar and salt. Beat the egg whites at high speed until they stand in peaks. Gently spread the egg whites over the pie filling, completely covering the filling to the edges of the crust. Slip into the broiler about 4 inches (10 cm) from the heat and broil (grill) for 1 or 2 minutes, or until the peaks are brown.

Makes topping for one 9-inch (23-cm) pie

Chocolate-Walnut Pastry

Like the preceding rich tart pastry, this cookielike dough may be pressed into a pie pan or tart pan with your fingers. For a quick dessert, fully bake and cool the shell, fill it with softened ice cream, and return it to the freezer to firm up. Serve it with whipped cream or chocolate sauce.

1 cup (4 oz/125 g) all-purpose (plain) flour
½ cup (2 oz/60 g) ground walnuts
⅓ cup (1½ oz/45 g) unsweetened cocoa
¼ cup (2 oz/60 g) sugar
¼ teaspoon salt
½ cup (4 oz/125 g) unsalted butter, chilled
¼ cup (2 fl oz/60 ml), or more, milk
1 teaspoon vanilla extract (essence)

Combine the flour, walnuts, cocoa, sugar and salt in a mixing bowl and toss to combine. Add the butter and blend it into the dry ingredients with a pastry blender or your fingertips. Add ¼ cup (2 fl oz/60 ml) milk and the vanilla and stir until the dough forms a cohesive mass. If it is too dry, add a few drops more milk.

   Press walnut-sized pieces of dough over the bottom and sides of a 9-inch (23-cm) pie or tart pan, taking care to make it even. (If you wish to roll the dough out, wrap it well in plastic wrap and chill for about 1 hour, then roll it out on a generously floured surface.) Follow the instructions on page 10 for partially and fully baked shells, depending upon the recipe.

Makes one 9-inch (23-cm) pie or tart shell

Whipped Cream

A good, fast finish for many pies and tarts, and it only takes a dollop to impart a wonderful dash of richness. But don't think of this cream only as a topping: Spread whipped cream in a fully baked tart shell and crown it with fresh figs, berries or peaches for a quick, simple dessert. The powdered milk is a stabilizer, to keep the cream from deflating. You can't taste it, but it works.

1 cup (8 fl oz/250 ml) heavy (double) cream, chilled
4 teaspoons sugar
1 tablespoon nonfat dry milk (milk powder)
1 teaspoon vanilla extract (essence)

Combine the cream, sugar, dry milk and vanilla in a mixing bowl and beat until the cream stands in soft peaks. If you plan to pipe the cream through a pastry bag, beat it until it stands in stiff peaks.

Makes about 2 cups (16 fl oz/500 ml)

Pastry Cream

Plain pastry cream is delicious spread in a baked tart shell and topped with ripe berries, sliced peaches or other fruit. You can flavor the cream with 1 ounce (30 g) melted unsweetened (cooking) chocolate, or with toasted grated coconut or toasted pulverized nuts.

1 cup (8 fl oz/250 ml) milk
¼ cup (2 oz/60 g) sugar
1½ tablespoons cornstarch (cornflour)
pinch of salt
2 egg yolks, lightly beaten
2 tablespoons unsalted butter
1 teaspoon vanilla extract (essence)

Bring the milk to a simmer in a heavy-bottomed saucepan. Meanwhile, in a mixing bowl stir together the sugar, cornstarch and salt. Gradually add the hot milk to the sugar mixture, whisking constantly. Pour the milk mixture back into the saucepan and cook over medium heat, stirring constantly, until the mixture boils and thickens slightly, 7–10 minutes. Whisk in the egg yolks, then cook, stirring, until slightly thicker, about 2 minutes longer. Remove the saucepan from the heat and stir in the butter.

Let cool to room temperature, stirring occasionally. Add the vanilla, cover and chill thoroughly. Pastry cream will keep in the refrigerator, tightly covered, for up to 3 days.

Makes about 1½ cups
(12 fl oz/375 ml)

Apricot Glaze

A coating of warm apricot glaze on a fruit tart makes it glisten. The classic method, in which the jam is sieved, makes a perfectly clear glaze, while the food processor version is faster and less wasteful, but not as sparkling. Glazes keep well tightly capped in the refrigerator.

1½ cups (16 oz/500 g) apricot jam

CLASSIC METHOD: Bring the jam to a boil in a small saucepan, stirring frequently. Place a strainer over a bowl and add the jam to the strainer. Using the back of a spoon, press it through the strainer to remove the pulp. Discard the pulp and return the strained jam to the saucepan. Reheat to a boil before using.

Makes about 1 cup (8 fl oz/250 ml)

FOOD PROCESSOR METHOD: Whirl the jam in a food processor until it is smooth. Bring to a boil in a saucepan, stirring frequently. The glaze is now ready to use.

Makes about 1½ cups (12 fl oz/375 ml)

Currant Glaze

Currant glaze is darker than apricot glaze, and perfectly clear. It is good on fresh red berries, such as raspberries and strawberries.

1 cup (11 oz/345 g) red currant jelly
1 tablespoon fresh lemon juice

Bring the jelly and lemon juice to a boil in a small saucepan, stirring frequently. Remove from the heat and let cool for a moment. The glaze is now ready to use. If the glaze thickens too much upon standing, reheat gently to liquefy it.

Makes about 1 cup (8 fl oz/250 ml)

Fig and Berry Tart

rich tart pastry for a 9-inch (23-cm) tart
  shell *(recipe on page 14)*
½–⅔ cup (4–5 fl oz/125–160 ml) pastry
  cream *(recipe on page 16)*
1 cup (4 oz/125 g) blueberries
1 cup (4 oz/125 g) blackberries or
  raspberries
6 figs, halved lengthwise
⅓ cup (4 oz/125 g) red currant jelly
1 teaspoon fresh lemon juice

This tart looks fancy, but it is actually easier to make than many plainer-looking pies. You can put it together even more quickly by substituting a layer of whipped cream for the pastry cream. Have all of the ingredients ready ahead of time, so that you can assemble the tart just before serving.

Preheat an oven to 425°F (220°C). Pat the pastry into a 9-inch (23-cm) tart pan (or roll it out). Bake the crust fully, until browned and crisp (see page 10 for detailed instructions). Cool completely before filling.

Spread a thin (¼-inch/6-mm) layer of pastry cream over the bottom of the cooled tart shell. Place the berries and figs atop the pastry cream, being as fancy or as casual as you wish with the arrangement.

In a small pan, combine the currant jelly and lemon juice and bring to a boil, stirring frequently. Let cool for a moment, then brush it on the fruit. Serve the tart as soon as possible after assembling.

Makes one 9-inch (23-cm) tart

Mango Chiffon Pie

crumb crust for a 9-inch (23-cm) pie
  shell, made with graham crackers
  (recipe on page 14)
2 large, ripe mangoes
¼ cup (2 fl oz/60 ml) water
1 envelope (1 tablespoon) unflavored
  gelatin
5 eggs, separated
2 tablespoons fresh lemon juice
½ cup (4 oz/125 g) sugar
1 teaspoon ground ginger
¼ teaspoon salt

*Mangoes have a remarkable refreshing quality unlike any
other fruit, and they make this pie rich and creamy, even
though there is no cream in it. You may substitute papayas
if you wish.*

❖

Preheat an oven to 325°F (165°C). Pat the crumb mixture
into a 9-inch (23-cm) pie pan and bake for 8 minutes. Cool
completely before filling.

Peel the mangoes and slice the flesh off the pit. Purée the
pulp in a food processor; you should have about 1½ cups
(12 fl oz/375 ml). Set the mango pulp aside. Place the water
in a small cup and sprinkle the gelatin over the top. Let
stand for a few minutes to soften.

Meanwhile, in a heavy-bottomed saucepan, whisk the egg
yolks with the lemon juice and ¼ cup (2 oz/60 g) of the
sugar. Cook over moderate heat for about 4 minutes,
whisking constantly, until the mixture is thick, foamy and
very hot. Do not let it boil. Add the softened gelatin and
whisk over heat about 30 seconds longer. Pour into a bowl
and stir in the mango purée and ginger. Chill, stirring
occasionally, until the mixture is the consistency of
unbeaten egg whites and mounds slightly when dropped
from a spoon.

Beat the egg whites with the salt until soft peaks form.
Add the remaining ¼ cup (2 oz/60 g) sugar and beat until
stiff. Gently fold the egg whites into the mango mixture. Pile
the filling into the crust and chill for several hours.

Makes one 9-inch (23-cm) single-crust pie

Berry-Cherry Pie

basic pie pastry for a 9-inch (23-cm)
  double-crust pie *(recipe on page 12)*
2 tablespoons quick-cooking tapioca
¾ cup (6 oz/185 g) sugar
¼ teaspoon salt
3 cups (12 oz/375 g) pitted sweet or
  sour cherries
3 cups (12 oz/375 g) raspberries,
  blackberries or boysenberries
2 tablespoons unsalted butter

*Cherries and berries of any type will make a good pie—
except for strawberries, which are best in their natural
state, in a tart for instance. If you have sour cherries,
increase the sugar to 1 cup (8 oz/250 g). A lattice top
provides a nice touch.*

Preheat an oven to 425°F (220°C). Roll out the pastry for
the bottom crust and use to line a 9-inch (23-cm) pie pan.
Roll out the pastry for the top crust and set it aside.

In a large bowl stir together the tapioca, sugar and salt.
Add the cherries and berries and toss to mix well. Pile the
fruit mixture into the pastry-lined pan and dot with bits of
the butter. Cover with the top crust and trim and flute the
edges. Cut a few vents in the top for steam to escape.

Bake for 25 minutes, then reduce the heat to 350°F
(180°C) and bake until the juices are bubbling and the crust
is browned, about 35 minutes longer.

Makes one 9-inch (23-cm) double-crust pie

23

Tropical Cream Pie

crumb crust for a 9-inch (23-cm) pie
   shell, made with graham crackers
   (recipe on page 14)
¼ cup (1 oz/30 g) all-purpose (plain)
   flour
⅔ cup (5 oz/155 g) sugar
¼ teaspoon salt
2 cups (16 fl oz/500 ml) milk
2 eggs, beaten
¼ cup (2 oz/60 g) unsalted butter
1 teaspoon vanilla extract (essence)
1 large, firm but ripe banana
1 firm but ripe papaya
1 tablespoon fresh lemon juice

*An old-fashioned vanilla filling with sliced banana and
papaya. Serve with whipped cream.*

❖

Preheat an oven to 325°F (165°C). Pat the crumb mixture
into a 9-inch (23-cm) pie pan and bake for 8 minutes. Cool
completely before filling.

Stir the flour, sugar and salt together; set aside. In a heavy-
bottomed saucepan, bring the milk to a simmer. Pour the
sugar mixture into the milk in a thin stream, whisking
constantly to keep the mixture smooth. Whisk in the eggs.
Cook over moderate heat, stirring or whisking constantly,
until it boils and thickens, 7–10 minutes. Reduce the heat
and boil gently for 3 minutes, stirring constantly. Remove
from the heat and add the butter, stirring until smooth.

Add the vanilla and mix well. Pour into a bowl and cover
with plastic wrap, pressing the wrap directly onto the
surface. Chill until set.

Shortly before serving, peel the banana, slice it crosswise
¼ inch (6 mm) thick and place the slices in a large bowl.
Peel the papaya, quarter it lengthwise and scoop out and
discard the seeds. Slice each quarter crosswise ¼ inch
(6 mm) thick. Save a few of the papaya slices to garnish the
pie and add the remaining papaya to the banana. Add the
lemon juice and toss to coat the fruit. Gently fold the fruit
into the chilled filling. Spread the mixture in the cooled
crust and garnish with the reserved papaya.

Makes one 9-inch (23-cm) single-crust pie

Simple Summer Tart

basic pie pastry for a 9-inch (23-cm)
   double-crust pie *(recipe on page 12)*
sugar
5–6 cups (1¼–1½ lb/600–750 g)
   prepared fruit *(see note, right)*
1 cup (8 fl oz/250 ml) heavy (double)
   cream or ½ pint (8 fl oz/250 ml)
   vanilla ice cream

A casual tart of thin, sugared pastry covered with fresh fruit. Make it any shape you wish—round, rectangular, square or uneven. You can bake the pastry in the morning, then top it with fruit just before serving. Use whole fresh berries or sliced peaches, plums or apricots, alone or in combination. In autumn, try sliced pears and kiwifruits.

Preheat an oven to 425°F (220°C). Prepare the pastry but form it into a single cake. Roll the pastry out about ⅛ inch (3 mm) thick in any shape you wish. Transfer the dough to a baking sheet and prick it all over with a fork. Fold up ½ inch (12 mm) of the dough all around to make a small rim. Bake the pastry sheet until golden brown and crisp, 15–20 minutes. Remove from the oven and sprinkle with 2 tablespoons sugar. Return the crust to the oven and bake for 1 minute longer. Remove from the oven once again, let cool on the baking sheet about 3 minutes, then carefully slide onto a rack and let cool completely.

To serve the tart, transfer the cooled pastry sheet to a large platter or board. Top with the prepared fruit, being as casual or as fancy as you wish with the arrangement. If the fruit is tart, sprinkle it with sugar. In a bowl combine the cream with sugar to taste and whip it to form soft peaks. Pass the cream with the tart. Or, if you wish, accompany the tart with vanilla ice cream.

Makes one free-form tart; serves 6–8

Blueberry-Cheese Pie

crumb crust for a 9-inch (23-cm) pie
shell, made with graham crackers
(*recipe on page 14*)

FOR THE CHEESE CUSTARD:
8 oz (250 g) cream cheese, at room
temperature
⅓ cup (3 oz/90 g) sugar
1 teaspoon vanilla extract (essence)
2 eggs

FOR THE BERRIES:
2 cups (8 oz/250 g) blueberries
½ cup (4 fl oz/125 ml) water
⅓ cup (3 oz/90 g) sugar
1½ tablespoons cornstarch (cornflour)
mixed with 2 tablespoons water

*This is similar to a blueberry cheesecake, but lighter and not
as rich. It uses a crumb crust, so there is no pastry to roll out,
and if you want to spend even less time in the kitchen, you
can substitute uncooked whole raspberries or sliced
strawberries for the blueberries.*

*P*reheat an oven to 325°F (165°C). Pat the crumb mixture
into a 9-inch (23-cm) pie pan and bake for 8 minutes. Cool
completely before filling.

Meanwhile, make the cheese custard: In a bowl combine
the cheese, sugar and vanilla and beat until thoroughly
mixed and smooth. Add the eggs and beat well. Pour into
the baked shell and bake until just set, 25–30 minutes.
Remove from the oven and let cool.

While the custard is cooking, combine the berries, water
and sugar in a saucepan and bring to a boil. Reduce the heat
and simmer, covered, for about 5 minutes, stirring once.
Remove from the heat and add the cornstarch and water
mixture. Bring back to a boil and cook for about 1 minute,
stirring constantly. Remove from the heat and let cool
until tepid.

Spoon the berries over the custard. Chill for at least 1
hour before serving.

Makes one 9-inch (23-cm) single-crust pie

Orange Meringue Pie

tart pastry for a 9-inch (23-cm) tart shell
  (recipe on page 13)
⅓ cup (3 oz/90 g) sugar
2 tablespoons cornstarch (cornflour)
¼ teaspoon salt
1½ cups (12 fl oz/375 ml) orange juice
5 egg yolks
3 tablespoons (2 oz/50 g) unsalted
  butter
1½ tablespoons freshly grated orange
  zest
meringue topping (recipe on page 15)

A thin layer of orange custard on buttery pastry topped with a soft meringue. A nice change from the familiar lemon meringue pie.

Preheat an oven to 425°F (220°C). Roll out the pastry and use to line a 9-inch (23-cm) pie pan. Bake the crust fully, until browned and crisp (see page 10 for detailed instructions). Cool completely before filling.

In a heavy-bottomed saucepan, stir together the sugar, cornstarch and salt. Add the orange juice and mix well. Place over moderate heat and cook, stirring constantly, until the mixture thickens and boils, 10–12 minutes. Remove from the heat, add the egg yolks all at once and whisk until blended. Bring back to a boil and cook, stirring constantly, for 2 minutes. Add the butter and orange zest. Spread the orange juice mixture in the cooled pie shell.

Preheat a broiler (griller). Prepare the meringue topping and gently spread it over the pie filling, completely covering the filling to the edges of the crust. Broil (grill) as directed in the topping recipe. Remove from the oven and let cool before serving.

Makes one 9-inch (23-cm) single-crust pie

Fresh Peach Pie

basic pie pastry for a 9-inch (23-cm)
   double-crust pie (recipe on page 12)
6 cups (1¼ lb/625 g) peeled, pitted and
   sliced peaches
2 tablespoons fresh lemon juice
¼ cup (1 oz/30 g) all-purpose (plain)
   flour
⅔ cup (5 oz/155 g) sugar
¼ teaspoon salt
pinch of ground nutmeg
2 tablespoons unsalted butter

One of the best pies you'll ever make, with a lattice top to show off the beautiful filling. For some reason, peaches taste even better when cooked.

*P*reheat an oven to 425°F (220°C). Roll out the pastry for the bottom crust and use to line a 9-inch (23-cm) pie pan. Roll out the pastry for the top crust and cut it into strips about ¾ inch (2 cm) wide; set aside.

Place the peaches in a large bowl. Sprinkle with the lemon juice and toss to coat well; set aside. In a small bowl stir together the flour, sugar, salt and nutmeg. Add to the peaches and toss to combine. Pile the fruit mixture into the pastry-lined pan and dot with bits of the butter.

Use the pastry strips to make a lattice top (see page 10 for detailed instructions). Trim and flute the edges.

Bake for 25 minutes, then reduce the heat to 350°F (180°C) and bake until the juices are bubbling and the top is browned, about 25 minutes longer.

Makes one 9-inch (23-cm) lattice-top pie

Strawberry and Lemon Curd Tart

FOR THE LEMON CURD:
5 egg yolks
½ cup (4 oz/125 g) sugar
¼ cup (2 fl oz/60 ml) fresh lemon juice
freshly grated zest of 2 lemons
6 tablespoons (3 oz/90 g) unsalted butter

tart pastry for a 9-inch (23-cm) tart shell
    (recipe on page 13)
4 cups (1 lb/500 g) strawberries,
    stemmed
⅓ cup (3 fl oz/80 ml) currant glaze
    (recipe on page 17), warm

Sweet strawberries heaped in a crisp crust make a beautiful tart, but a thin layer of lemon curd between the pastry and berries transforms it into something truly special. Lemon curd also makes a delectable cake or cookie filling, and it keeps in the refrigerator for up to 10 days. If you wish, you can lighten the lemon curd by folding in whipped cream or beaten egg whites.

❖

*T*o make the lemon curd, combine the egg yolks and sugar in a heavy-bottomed saucepan. Whisk vigorously for 1 minute. Add the lemon juice and zest and whisk 1 minute more. Place over low heat and cook, stirring constantly, until slightly thickened; don't let it become too hot or the yolks will scramble. Remove from the heat and add the butter. Stir until smooth. Let cool, stirring occasionally. There should be about 1 cup (11 oz/345 g). Transfer to a tightly capped jar and chill before assembling the tart.

Preheat an oven to 425°F (220°C). Roll out the pastry and use to line a 9-inch (23-cm) tart pan. Bake the crust fully, until browned and crisp (see page 10 for detailed instructions). Cool completely before filling.

Spread the lemon curd in the cooled tart shell. If the strawberries are large, slice each one lengthwise into 2 or 3 pieces. Arrange the strawberries on top of the lemon curd. Brush with the warm currant glaze. Serve the tart as soon as possible.

Makes one 9-inch (23-cm) tart

Rhubarb-Raspberry Pie

basic pie pastry for a 9-inch (23-cm)
  double-crust pie *(recipe on page 12)*
1 cup (8 oz/250 g) sugar
3 tablespoons (1 oz/30 g) cornstarch
  (cornflour)
¼ teaspoon salt
1¼ lb (625 g) rhubarb stalks, peeled and
  sliced into ½-inch (12-mm) pieces,
  about 4 cups (1 lb/500 g)
2 cups (8 oz/250 g) raspberries
2 tablespoons unsalted butter

Select a different berry if you wish, depending on what is available. Blackberries, loganberries and boysenberries would all be a good choice, although you may need to increase the sugar if they are very tart. Rhubarb, because it makes a wonderful pie and is often the first harvest from a spring garden, is sometimes called pie plant. Be sure to use only the stalks, as the leaves and roots are toxic. Serve a wedge of this delectable pie with a spoonful of crème fraîche, sour cream or whipped cream.

Preheat an oven to 425°F (220°C). Roll out the pastry for the bottom crust and use to line a 9-inch (23-cm) pie pan. Roll out the pastry for the top crust and set it aside.

In a large bowl stir together the sugar, cornstarch and salt. Add the rhubarb and raspberries and toss to mix well. Pile the fruit mixture into the pastry-lined pan and dot with bits of the butter. Cover with the top crust and trim and flute the edges. Cut a few vents in the top for steam to escape.

Bake for 20 minutes, then reduce the heat to 350°F (180°C) and bake until the juices are bubbling and the crust is browned, 30–40 minutes longer.

Makes one 9-inch (23-cm) double-crust pie

Deep-Dish Plum Pie

basic pie pastry for a 9-inch (23-cm) pie
shell (recipe on page 12)

1½ cups (12 oz/375 g) sugar

¼ cup (1 oz/30 g) all-purpose (plain)
flour

¼ teaspoon salt

8 cups (2 lb/1 kg) peeled, pitted and
quartered plums (about 4 lb/2 kg
whole)

1 tablespoon fresh lemon juice

3 tablespoons unsalted butter

1 tablespoon heavy (double) cream

*Deep-dish pies are bountiful, made with a large amount of
fruit and baked in a casserole or soufflé dish with only a top
crust. The shape of the dish isn't critical, but the sides must
be at least 3 inches (7.5 cm) tall, so the juices don't boil over
them. Because there is no bottom crust to get soggy, deep-dish
pies reheat perfectly the next day.*

Preheat an oven to 425°F (220°C). You will need a baking
dish of about 8-cup (64-fl oz/2-l) capacity and about 3
inches (7.5 cm) deep. Roll out the pastry to a shape about
1 inch (2.5 cm) larger than the top of the baking dish.

In a large bowl stir together the sugar, flour and salt.
Add the plums and lemon juice and toss to mix well. Pile
the plum mixture in the baking dish and dot with bits of the
butter. Cover the top with the pastry. Fold the overhanging
pastry under itself to make a double-thick edge, then flute
the edge. Brush the crust with the cream. Cut a few vents in
the top for steam to escape.

Bake until the crust is browned and the fruit is tender
when pierced with a knife inserted through a vent, 50–60
minutes.

Makes one deep-dish pie; serves 8

Strawberry and Blueberry Pie

basic pie pastry for a 9-inch (23-cm) pie
   shell *(recipe on page 12)*
⅔ cup (5 oz/155 g) sugar
2 tablespoons cornstarch (cornflour)
4 cups (1 lb/500 g) strawberries,
   stemmed
2 tablespoons fresh lemon juice
2 cups (8 oz/250 g) blueberries
⅓ cup (3 fl oz/80 ml) currant glaze or
   apricot glaze *(recipe on page 17)*, warm

*Add whipped cream topping to make this red and blue
pie an even more colorful dessert.*

Preheat an oven to 425°F (220°C). Roll out the pastry and
use to line a 9-inch (23-cm) pie pan. Bake the crust fully,
until browned and crisp (see page 10 for detailed
instructions). Cool completely before filling.

   Stir the sugar and cornstarch together in a saucepan.
Add 2 cups (8 oz/250 g) of the strawberries and the lemon
juice and mash the berries with a potato masher. Place over
moderate heat and cook, stirring constantly, until the
mixture boils. Reduce the heat to low and cook gently for
2 minutes. Remove from the heat and let cool until tepid,
stirring occasionally.

   Fold 1½ cups (6 oz/190 g) of the blueberries into the
strawberry mixture and spread it in the cooled pie shell.
Arrange the remaining 2 cups (8 oz/250 g) strawberries
around the edge of the pie and fill the center with the
remaining ½ cup (2 oz/60 g) blueberries. Brush the glaze
over the fruit.

Makes one 9-inch (23-cm) single-crust pie

Apricot-Pineapple Pie

basic pie pastry for a 9-inch (23-cm)
   double-crust pie *(recipe on page 12)*
1 ripe pineapple
⅔ cup (5 oz/155 g) sugar
2 tablespoons quick-cooking tapioca
¼ teaspoon ground nutmeg
pinch of salt
3 cups (12 oz/375 g) pitted and
   quartered apricots
2 tablespoons unsalted butter

Because of an enzyme it contains, fresh pineapple isn't too successful in breads and cakes, although it makes a very good pie. The filling is generous and quite juicy, so put a foil-lined baking sheet on the oven shelf below to catch any drips. This pie can also be made with a lattice top to show off the fruit filling.

❖

Preheat an oven to 425°F (220°C). Roll out the pastry for the bottom crust and use to line a 9-inch (23-cm) pie pan. Roll out the pastry for the top crust and set it aside.

Peel the pineapple, cutting deeply enough to remove all the prickly "eyes." Quarter it lengthwise, then cut out and discard the fibrous core from each piece. Cut each quarter in half lengthwise, then cut the pieces crosswise into slices ¼ inch (6 mm) thick.

In a large bowl stir together the sugar, tapioca, nutmeg and salt. Add the pineapple and apricots and toss to mix well. Pile the pineapple mixture in the pastry-lined pan and dot with bits of the butter. Cover with the top crust and trim and flute the edges. Cut a few vents in the top for steam to escape.

Bake for 25 minutes, then reduce the heat to 350°F (180°C) and bake until the juices are bubbling and the crust is browned, 30–40 minutes longer.

Makes one 9-inch (23-cm) double-crust pie

Cherry-Almond Pie

basic pie pastry for a 9-inch (23-cm)
  double-crust pie *(recipe on page 12)*
⅓ cup (2 oz/60 g) toasted almonds
⅔ cup (5 oz/155 g) sugar, if using sweet
  cherries, or 1⅓ cups (10 oz/310 g),
  if using sour
3 tablespoons (1 oz/30 g) cornstarch
  (cornflour)
5 cups (1¼ lb/625 g) pitted sweet or
  sour cherries
¼ teaspoon salt
2 tablespoons unsalted butter

*Sour cherries make a great pie, but they can be difficult to
find, depending upon where you live. If you are able to use
them, increase the amount of sugar to 1⅓ cups (10 oz/310 g).
Almonds give the filling added texture, and they complement
the cherry flavor. A lattice top shows off the colorful filling.*

*P*reheat an oven to 425°F (220°C). Roll out the pastry
for the bottom crust and use to line a 9-inch (23-cm) pie
pan. Roll out the pastry for the top crust and cut it into
strips about ¾ inch (2 cm) wide; set aside.

In a food processor or blender, combine the almonds,
sugar and cornstarch. Whirl until the nuts are pulverized.
Place the cherries in a large bowl, add the sugar mixture and
salt and toss to mix well. Pile the cherry mixture into the
pastry-lined pan and dot with bits of the butter.

Use the pastry strips to make a lattice top (see page 10 for
detailed instructions). Trim and flute the edges.

Bake for 25 minutes, then reduce the heat to 350°F
(180°C) and bake until the juices are bubbling and the top
is browned, about 35 minutes longer.

Makes one 9-inch (23-cm) lattice-top pie

Apple-Pear Pie

basic pie pastry for a 9-inch (23-cm)
   double-crust pie *(recipe on page 12)*
3 large, firm but ripe pears, peeled,
   cored and sliced
3 large apples, peeled, cored and sliced
2 tablespoons fresh lemon juice
½ cup (3 oz/90 g) firmly packed brown
   sugar
3 tablespoons all-purpose (plain) flour
½ teaspoon ground cinnamon
¼ teaspoon salt
3 tablespoons dry or sweet sherry
2 tablespoons unsalted butter
1 tablespoon heavy (double) cream
1 tablespoon raw sugar or granulated
   sugar

Pears and apples are an especially good combination, and a blend of sherry and cinnamon brings out the flavor of the fruits. This pie is nice with a wedge of good blue cheese.

❤

Preheat an oven to 425°F (220°C). Roll out the pastry for the bottom crust and use to line a 9-inch (23-cm) pie pan. Roll out the pastry for the top crust and set it aside.

   In a large bowl combine the pears and apples. Add the lemon juice and toss to coat the fruit. In a small bowl stir together the brown sugar, flour, cinnamon and salt. Add to the fruit and toss to combine. Add the sherry and toss until completely mixed. Pile the fruit into the pastry-lined pan and dot with bits of the butter. Cover with the top crust and trim and flute the edges. Cut a few vents in the top for steam to escape. Brush the top crust with the cream and sprinkle with the sugar.

   Bake for 30 minutes, then reduce the heat to 350°F (180°C) and bake until the crust is browned and the fruit is tender when pierced with a knife inserted through a vent, about 35 minutes longer.

Makes one 9-inch (23-cm) double-crust pie

Free-Form Apple Tart

basic pie pastry for a 9-inch (23-cm)
   double-crust pie *(recipe on page 12)*
4 large apples, preferably Golden
   Delicious
3 tablespoons sugar
2 tablespoons unsalted butter
1 teaspoon vanilla extract (essence)
½ cup (2 oz/60 g) chopped pistachios
½ cup (4 fl oz/125 ml) apricot glaze
   (recipe on page 17), warm

Not all tarts are baked in pans. This one is done free-form, with just sugared apples baked on a rectangle of pastry. Try other fruits, too, such as sliced pears or peaches. They must be ripe but firm; fruits that are soft and juicy will make the pastry soggy.

*P*at the pastry dough into a rectangular rather than a round cake, wrap in plastic wrap and chill for about 30 minutes. Cover a baking sheet with aluminum foil and butter the foil.

Roll out the dough into a rectangle about 18 inches (45 cm) long and 6 inches (15 cm) wide, keeping the border as even as possible. Trim the edges to make them even and to make the corners square. Transfer the dough to the prepared baking sheet. Paint the edges of the dough with cold water, then fold ½ inch (12 mm) of the edge under all around, to form a slight ridge. With your fingertips or the tines of a fork, press the ridge down firmly all around; refrigerate.

Preheat an oven to 400°F (200°C). Peel, halve and core the apples. Cut each apple half into slices about ³⁄₁₆ inch (4 mm) thick, keeping the slices in the shape of the apple half. Arrange lengthwise on the pastry, fanning the slices slightly. Sprinkle on the sugar, dot with bits of the butter and then drizzle with the vanilla. Strew the pistachios evenly over the top. Bake until the fruit is tender when pierced with a knife and the crust is browned, about 45 minutes.

Let cool for a moment, then slide the tart onto a board or platter. Brush with the warm apricot glaze.

Makes one free-form tart; serves 6–8

Rhubarb Crisp Pie

basic pie pastry for a 9-inch (23-cm) pie
   shell *(recipe on page 12)*

FOR THE FILLING:
1½ lb (750 g) rhubarb stalks
¼ cup (2 fl oz/60 ml) water
3 tablespoons all-purpose (plain) flour
¾ cup (6 oz/185 g) sugar

FOR THE TOPPING:
¼ cup (2 oz/60 g) unsalted butter, at
   room temperature
½ cup (4 oz/125 g) sugar
½ cup (2 oz/60 g) all-purpose (plain)
   flour
½ cup (2 oz/60 g) uncooked oatmeal
   (rolled oats)
½ teaspoon ground cardamom

*Here is one of the very best ways to use fresh rhubarb.
It becomes soft but not mushy, and its tart flavor is comple-
mented by the sweet topping.*

♥

Preheat an oven to 350°F (180°C). Roll out the pastry
and use to line a 9-inch (23-cm) pie pan. Set aside.

Trim the rhubarb stalks and cut them into 1-inch
(2.5-cm) pieces; you should have about 5 cups (1¼ lb/
625 g). Place them in a saucepan with the water. In a small
bowl stir together the flour and sugar and add to the
rhubarb. Bring just to a boil, then reduce the heat and
simmer partially covered until barely tender, about 5
minutes; do not cook the rhubarb until it is mushy. Set the
rhubarb aside while you prepare the topping.

Combine the butter, sugar, flour, oatmeal and cardamom
in a mixing bowl. With your fingertips blend together the
ingredients until the mixture resembles coarse crumbs.

Spread the rhubarb in the pie shell and sprinkle with the
topping. Bake until the juices are bubbling and the crust is
browned, about 40 minutes.

Makes one 9-inch (23-cm) single-crust pie

Fresh Pineapple Cream Pie

2 cups (8 oz/250 g) cubed (½ inch/
   12 mm) fresh pineapple
½ cup (4 fl oz/125 ml) maple syrup
basic pie pastry for a 9-inch (23-cm) pie
   shell (*recipe on page 12*)
⅓ cup (3 oz/90 g) sugar
5 tablespoons (1½ oz/45 g) cornstarch
   (cornflour)
¼ teaspoon salt
2½ cups (20 fl oz/625 ml) milk
4 egg yolks
¼ cup (2 oz/60 g) unsalted butter,
   at room temperature
1 teaspoon vanilla extract (essence)
meringue topping (*recipe on page 15*)

Fresh pineapple, simmered in maple syrup and folded into vanilla pudding, makes a sweet and delicious filling.

❤

Combine the pineapple and maple syrup in a saucepan. Place over moderate heat and bring to a simmer. Cover and cook gently until the fruit is tender, about 10 minutes. Remove from the heat and let sit for 30 minutes. Pour into the work bowl of a food processor and process to chop coarsely. Set aside.

Preheat an oven to 425°F (220°C). Roll out the pastry and use to line a 9-inch (23-cm) pie pan. Bake the crust fully, until browned and crisp (see page 10 for detailed instructions). Cool completely before filling.

In a heavy-bottomed saucepan, stir together the sugar, cornstarch and salt. Add the milk and whisk until smooth. Place over moderate heat and cook, stirring or whisking constantly, until the mixture boils. Cook for 2 minutes, then stir in the egg yolks. Return to a boil, then reduce the heat and continue to cook, stirring, for 2 minutes more. Add the reserved pineapple and syrup and cook 1 minute longer. Remove from the heat and stir in the butter and vanilla. Cool for 20 minutes, then spread in the cooled pie shell.

Preheat a broiler (griller). Prepare the meringue topping and gently spread it over the pie filling, completely covering the filling to the edge of the crust. Broil (grill) as directed in the topping recipe.

Makes one 9-inch (23-cm) single-crust pie

Poached Pear Tart

FOR THE PEARS:

2 cups (16 fl oz/500 ml) dry red wine

¾ cup (6 oz/185 g) sugar

1 cinnamon stick, about 2 inches (5 cm)

3 whole cloves

5 firm but ripe pears, preferably Boscs

rich tart pastry for a 9-inch (23-cm) tart
shell (*recipe on page 14*)

½ cup (4 fl oz/125 ml) apricot glaze
(*recipe on page 17*), warm

⅓ cup (3 fl oz/80 ml) heavy (double)
cream

2 teaspoons sugar

1 teaspoon nonfat dry milk (milk
powder)

1 teaspoon vanilla extract (essence) or
2 tablespoons pear brandy

Everyone loves this tart of glistening pear halves on whipped cream–cloaked pastry. It is also good in a meringue shell (recipe on page 76), for a tart of interesting textures and flavors.

❤

To cook the pears, combine the red wine, sugar, cinnamon stick and cloves in a medium saucepan and bring to a boil. Reduce the heat and simmer, partially covered, for 5 minutes. Peel, halve and core the pears. Place them in the simmering liquid, adding a little water if necessary to cover them completely with liquid. Poach gently until tender when pierced with a knife, about 15 minutes. Remove from the heat and let the pears cool in the liquid for at least 2 hours, or for up to several days in the refrigerator.

Preheat an oven to 425°F (220°C). Press the pastry into a 9-inch (23-cm) tart pan (or roll it out). Bake the crust fully, until browned and crisp (see page 10 for detailed instructions). Cool completely before filling.

Remove the pears from the poaching liquid and pat them dry. Brush a thin coating of the warm apricot glaze over the bottom of the cooled tart shell. In a bowl combine the cream, sugar and dry milk and beat until stiff. Flavor with the vanilla or pear brandy. Spread the whipped cream in an even layer in the tart shell. Arrange the pear halves on the cream, cut side down and small end toward the center. Place 1 or 2 halves in the middle of the tart to cover the center. Carefully brush the pear halves with the remaining apricot glaze and serve as soon as possible.

Makes one 9-inch (23-cm) tart

Cranberry-Apple Pie

basic pie pastry for a 9-inch (23-cm)
  double-crust pie (recipe on page 12)
1 cup (8 oz/250 g) sugar
2 tablespoons all-purpose (plain) flour
¼ teaspoon salt
2 cups (8 oz/250 g) cranberries
½ cup (3 oz/90 g) raisins
4 tart apples, preferably Pippin or
  Granny Smith, peeled, cored and
  thinly sliced
freshly grated zest of 1 orange
2 tablespoons unsalted butter

Crisp apple slices combined with the color and tartness of fresh cranberries make a pie that is appropriate for any holiday dinner. Firm pears, like Boscs, may be substituted for the apples.

❤

Preheat an oven to 425°F (220°C). Roll out the pastry for the bottom crust and use to line a 9-inch (23-cm) pie pan. Roll out the pastry for the top crust and set it aside.

In a large bowl stir together the sugar, flour and salt. Add the cranberries, raisins, apples and orange zest and toss to mix well. Pile the fruit mixture into the pastry-lined pan and dot with bits of the butter. Cover with the top crust and trim and flute the edges. Cut a few vents in the top for steam to escape.

Bake for 20 minutes, then reduce the heat to 350°F (180°C) and bake until the crust is browned and the fruit is tender when pierced with a knife inserted through a vent, 40–50 minutes longer.

Makes one 9-inch (23-cm) double-crust pie

Quince Tart

tart pastry for a 9-inch (23-cm) tart
   shell *(recipe on page 13)*
2½ cups (20 fl oz/625 ml) water
1½ cups (12 oz/375 g) sugar
1 cinnamon stick, about 2 inches (5 cm)
1 teaspoon freshly grated lemon zest
3 quinces
½ cup (5 oz/155 g) apricot jam

Uncooked quinces are harsh tasting, but simmering them in sugar syrup transforms them, turning the flavor sweet and delicate. Serve this tart with whipped cream.

♥

Preheat an oven to 425°F (220°C). Roll out the pastry and use to line a 9-inch (23-cm) tart pan. Bake fully, until browned and crisp (see page 10 for detailed instructions). Cool completely before filling.

Combine the water, sugar, cinnamon stick and lemon zest in a saucepan. Bring to a boil over moderate heat, stirring until the sugar dissolves. Turn the heat to low while you prepare the fruit.

Peel, halve and core each quince—just as you would an apple. Cut each half into 4 wedges. Drop into the simmering sugar syrup and cook, partially covered, until tender but not mushy, 15–20 minutes. Remove from the heat and let cool completely. Drain the quinces well, reserving the liquid. Pat them dry with absorbent paper towels.

Cut each wedge lengthwise into 2 or 3 slices; set aside. In a small, heavy-bottomed saucepan, combine the apricot jam with ¼ cup (2 fl oz/60 ml) of the reserved quince liquid. Place over high heat and boil until thick and syrupy, which should take several minutes. Pass the syrup through a fine-mesh sieve to remove the pulp. Brush a thin coating of the warm sieved glaze over the bottom of the cooled tart shell. Arrange the quince attractively in the tart shell, overlapping the slices. Carefully brush with the remaining glaze and serve as soon as possible.

Makes one 9-inch (23-cm) tart

Spiced Applesauce Pie

basic pie pastry for a 9-inch (23-cm) pie
   shell (recipe on page 12)

FOR THE FILLING:
4 tart apples, preferably Pippin or
   Granny Smith, peeled, cored and cut
   into small pieces
¼ cup (2 fl oz/60 ml) water
½ cup (4 oz/125 g) sugar
2 eggs
¾ cup (6 fl oz/180 ml) heavy (double)
   cream
½ teaspoon ground cinnamon
2 tablespoons unsalted butter, melted
¼ teaspoon salt

FOR THE TOPPING:
3 tablespoons unsalted butter, softened
½ cup (3 oz/90 g) firmly packed brown
   sugar
½ cup (2 oz/60 g) uncooked oatmeal
   (rolled oats)
⅓ cup (1½ oz/45 g) all-purpose (plain)
   flour
½ cup (2 oz/60 g) coarsely chopped
   blanched almonds
pinch of salt

*An old-fashioned pie of spiced apple custard, perked up with
the texture of a crumbly topping.*

♥

Roll out the pastry and use to line a 9-inch (23-cm) pie
pan. Bake the crust partially until the pastry looks dry but is
still very pale (see page 10 for detailed instructions).

To make the filling, combine the apples and water in a
saucepan. Place over moderate heat, cover and cook,
stirring and mashing occasionally, until you have a thick
applesauce, 20–30 minutes. A few small lumps are okay.
Remove from the heat and pour into a large mixing bowl.
Let cool for 10 minutes.

Preheat an oven to 425°F (220°C). Add the sugar, eggs,
cream, cinnamon, butter and salt to the applesauce and
beat in to mix thoroughly. Pour the apple mixture into the
cooled pie shell and place the pie in the oven. While the pie
bakes, make the topping.

In a medium bowl combine the butter, sugar, oatmeal,
flour, almonds and salt. With your fingertips rub the
ingredients together until the mixture resembles coarse
crumbs. After the pie has been baking for 15 minutes,
rapidly sprinkle it with the topping mixture, then reduce
the heat to 350°F (180°C) and bake until the filling is set,
about 30 minutes longer.

Makes one 9-inch (23-cm) single-crust pie

Apple–Walnut Custard Tart

tart pastry for a 9-inch (23-cm) tart shell
   (recipe on page 13)
¼ cup (2 oz/60 g) unsalted butter
⅓ cup (3 oz/90 g) sugar
3 large apples, preferably Golden
   Delicious, peeled, cored and cut into
   ½-inch (12-mm) dice

FOR THE WALNUT CUSTARD:
¼ cup (scant 1 oz/30 g) walnuts,
   pulverized, plus ½ cup (2 oz/60 g)
   chopped walnuts
1 egg
2 tablespoons sugar
½ cup (4 fl oz/125 ml) heavy (double)
   cream
1 teaspoon vanilla extract (essence) or
   1 tablespoon Calvados
¼ teaspoon salt
⅓ cup (3 fl oz/80 ml) apricot glaze
   (recipe on page 17), warm

This tart of caramelized apples in a sweet walnut custard is a little more work than some of the others, but well worth the effort for a special occasion. It may also be made with firm pears such as Boscs.

♥

Preheat an oven to 425°F (220°C). Roll out the pastry and use to line a 9-inch (23-cm) tart pan. Bake the crust fully, until browned and crisp (see page 10 for detailed instructions). Cool completely before filling. Reduce the heat to 350°F (180°C).

Combine the butter and sugar in a large skillet and cook over moderate heat, stirring constantly, until melted and bubbling, then cook for 2 minutes more, stirring constantly. Add the apples and cook, stirring and tossing frequently, until they are slightly golden and any juices have evaporated, about 8 minutes. Spread the apple mixture in the cooled tart shell.

To make the custard, in a bowl whisk together the pulverized walnuts, egg, sugar, cream, vanilla or Calvados and salt. Pour over the apples. Sprinkle the chopped walnuts on top and bake until the custard is set, about 25 minutes.

Remove from the oven and let cool for 30 minutes. Brush the top with the warm apricot glaze.

Makes one 9-inch (23-cm) tart

Persimmon Chiffon Pie

crumb crust for a 9-inch (23-cm) pie
  shell, made with gingersnaps (recipe
  on page 14)
3 large ripe Hachiya persimmons
1 envelope (1 tablespoon) unflavored
  gelatin
¼ cup (2 fl oz/60 ml) water
4 eggs, separated
1 cup (8 oz/250 g) sugar
1 teaspoon ground cinnamon
1 teaspoon ground ginger
½ teaspoon ground nutmeg
¼ teaspoon salt
1 cup (8 fl oz/250 ml) heavy (double)
  cream

*Most persimmon concoctions are heavy and puddinglike.
This pie is light and spicy, with a good persimmon flavor.*

♥

Preheat an oven to 325°F (165°C). Press the crumb mixture
into a 9-inch (23-cm) pie pan and bake for 8 minutes. Cool
completely before filling.

Cut the persimmons in half and scoop out their flesh.
Purée in a food processor until smooth; you should have
1¼–1½ cups (10–12 fl oz/310–375 ml); set aside.

In a small bowl sprinkle the gelatin over the water and let
stand for a few minutes. In a heavy-bottomed saucepan,
place the egg yolks and whisk them for a moment. Add
¾ cup (6 oz/185 g) of the sugar, the cinnamon, ginger,
nutmeg, salt and persimmon purée. Cook over moderate
heat, whisking constantly, until the mixture thickens
slightly, 5–10 minutes; do not allow it to boil.

Stir in the softened gelatin and cook about 1 minute
longer, whisking constantly. Pour the mixture into a bowl
and refrigerate, stirring occasionally, until it mounds when
dropped from a spoon and is the consistency of unbeaten
egg whites, about 1 hour.

Whip the cream until stiff. In another bowl and with
clean beaters, beat the egg whites until soft peaks form.
Slowly add the remaining ¼ cup (2 oz/65 g) sugar and
continue beating until stiff peaks form. Fold the beaten
whites and whipped cream into the persimmon mixture
and pile into the prepared shell. Chill several hours.

Makes one 9-inch (23-cm) single-crust pie

Grape Tart

rich tart pastry for a 9-inch (23-cm) tart
    shell *(recipe on page 14)*
1½ lb (750 g), more or less, seedless
    grapes
½ cup (4 oz/125 ml) apricot glaze
    (recipe on page 17), warm
⅓ cup (3 fl oz/80 ml) heavy (double)
    cream
2 teaspoons sugar
1 tablespoon kirsch or brandy

Everyone is surprised at how good this is, and it's not only beautiful, it's uncomplicated. Use a mixture of red and green seedless grapes if you can, and assemble the tart as close to serving as possible.

♥

*P*reheat an oven to 425°F (220°C). Press the pastry into a 9-inch (23-cm) tart pan (or roll it out). Bake the crust fully, until browned and crisp (see page 10 for detailed instructions). Cool completely before filling.

Rinse and stem the grapes, discarding any that are bruised or mushy. Spread them on absorbent paper towels to dry thoroughly.

Brush a thin coating of the warm apricot glaze over the bottom of the cooled tart shell. In a bowl combine the cream, sugar and kirsch and beat until stiff. Spread the whipped cream in an even layer in the tart shell. Arrange the grapes in an attractive pattern—such as concentric circles—over the cream. Carefully brush the grapes with the remaining apricot glaze.

Makes one 9-inch (23-cm) tart

Apple Crumble Pie

FOR THE STREUSEL TOPPING:

1 cup (4 oz/125 g) all-purpose (plain)
  flour
½ cup (4 oz/125 g) sugar
¼ teaspoon salt
6 tablespoons (3 oz/90 g) unsalted
  butter, chilled

FOR THE PASTRY AND FILLING:

basic pie pastry for a 9-inch (23-cm) pie
  shell *(recipe on page 12)*
⅓ cup (3 oz/90 g) sugar
2 tablespoons all-purpose (plain) flour
½ teaspoon ground cinnamon
¼ teaspoon ground nutmeg
7 large tart apples, peeled, cored and
  thinly sliced
½ cup (3 oz/90 g) golden raisins
1 tablespoon fresh lemon juice

Instead of a top crust, this pie has a sweet, crunchy covering of streusel. The topping can be made in quantity— it keeps in the freezer for months—and is also good over peaches and apricots.

❤

Preheat an oven to 450°F (230°C). To make the topping, combine the flour, sugar and salt in a mixing bowl and stir together. Cut the butter into tablespoon-sized pieces and add them to the flour mixture. With your fingertips, two knives or a pastry blender, work the ingredients together until you have a mixture of fine, irregular crumbs. Set aside.

Roll out the pastry and use to line a 9-inch (23-cm) pie pan. Combine the sugar, flour, cinnamon and nutmeg. Add the apples, raisins and lemon juice and toss to combine. Pile the fruit mixture in the pastry-lined pan and spread the streusel mixture evenly over the top.

Bake for 20 minutes, then reduce the heat to 350°F (180°C) and bake until the crust is browned and the apples are tender when pierced with a knife, 35–45 minutes more.

Makes one 9-inch (23-cm) single-crust pie

Orange Tart

tart pastry for a 9-inch (23-cm) tart shell
(recipe on page 13)
3 oranges, preferably seedless and
unblemished
1 cup (8 oz/250 g) sugar
¼ cup (2 fl oz/60 ml) light corn syrup
1 cup (8 fl oz/250 ml) water
1 cinnamon stick, about 2 inches
(5 cm), broken into pieces
4 whole cloves
½ cup (4 fl oz/125 ml) pastry cream
(recipe on page 16)
½ cup (5 oz/155 g) orange marmalade
1 tablespoon freshly grated orange
zest

*Just glazed orange slices arranged atop pastry cream in
a tart shell—simple and gorgeous.*

❤

Preheat an oven to 425°F (220°C). Roll out the pastry and use to line a 9-inch (23-cm) tart pan. Bake the crust fully, until browned and crisp (see page 10 for detailed instructions). Cool completely before filling.

Place the oranges in a large saucepan and add water to cover. Bring to a boil, then reduce the heat to a simmer and cook until tender but not mushy when pierced, 15–20 minutes. Drain and let cool. Cut into slices ⅛–¼ inch (3 mm–6 mm) thick. Discard the end slices; pick out any seeds.

Combine the sugar, corn syrup, water, cinnamon stick and cloves in a saucepan. Place over high heat and boil for 5 minutes. Add the orange slices and reduce the heat. Boil very gently, swirling the pan now and then, until the syrup is thick and the oranges are very tender, about 1 hour or more. Remove from the heat and cool completely.

With a slotted utensil carefully lift the orange slices from the syrup, taking care not to break them; reserve the syrup. Spread the pastry cream in the tart shell and arrange the orange slices on top, overlapping them slightly. Combine ¼ cup (2 fl oz/60 ml) of the reserved cooking syrup and the orange marmalade in a small saucepan and boil over high heat until thick, a few minutes. Strain to remove the pulp. Stir the orange zest into the strained glaze. Brush the glaze over the oranges and serve at once.

Makes one 9-inch (23-cm) tart

Coconut Cream Tart

tart pastry for a 9-inch (23-cm) tart shell
  (recipe on page 13)
2½ cups (7 oz/225 g) packaged grated
  coconut
1 cup (8 fl oz/250 ml) water, boiling
½ cup (4 oz/125 g) sugar
1 tablespoon cornstarch (cornflour)
¼ teaspoon salt
1 cup (8 fl oz/250 ml) milk
4 egg yolks
6 tablespoons (3 oz/90 g) unsalted butter
1 teaspoon vanilla extract (essence)
whipped cream (recipe on page 16)

Packaged coconut is good but it is usually presweetened. You can remove some of the sugar by rinsing it under running water, then squeezing it dry, a handful at a time.

♥

Preheat an oven to 425°F (220°C). Roll out the pastry and use to line a 9-inch (23-cm) tart pan. Bake the crust fully, until browned and crisp (see page 10 for detailed instructions). Cool completely before filling. Reduce the oven temperature to 350°F (180°C).

Place 1½ cups (4 oz/140 g) of the grated coconut in a bowl. Pour in the boiling water and let stand for 30 minutes. Pour the mixture into a strainer placed over a bowl and press firmly on the coconut to extract every bit of liquid. Discard the used coconut. While the coconut is soaking, spread the remaining 1 cup (3 oz/90 g) coconut on a baking sheet and toast in the oven, stirring occasionally, until lightly browned, about 20 minutes; set aside.

In a saucepan, stir together the sugar, cornstarch and salt. Whisk in the milk and the reserved coconut liquid. Bring to a boil over moderate heat, stirring constantly. Remove from the heat and whisk in the egg yolks, then cook and stir about 3 minutes more. Remove from the heat and stir in the butter and then the vanilla. Blend in ¾ cup (2 oz/60 g) of the toasted coconut and let cool until tepid. Spread the mixture evenly in the tart shell and let cool completely.

Garnish with whipped cream and sprinkle with the remaining ¼ cup (1 oz/30 g) toasted coconut.

Makes one 9-inch (23-cm) tart

Pumpkin Pecan Pie
1½ cups pumpkin puree
_ cup toasted pecans
_ eggs
_ sugar

Pumpkin-Pecan Pie

basic pie pastry for a 9-inch (23-cm) pie
    shell *(recipe on page 12)*
1½ cups (1 lb/500 g) pumpkin purée
½ cup (1½ oz/45 g) toasted pecan halves
4 eggs
¾ cup (6 oz/185 g) sugar
¼ cup (2 fl oz/60 ml) rum
1 teaspoon ground cinnamon
1 teaspoon ground ginger
½ teaspoon ground cloves
1½ cups (12 fl oz/375 ml) heavy
    (double) cream

The amount of filling for this pie is generous, and some pie pans may not be deep enough to hold all of it. Form a high fluted edge, and if you still can't get all the filling in, bake the remainder in a small dish or custard cup. The pumpkin mixture, laced with rum and toasted pecans, is smooth, creamy and delicately spiced. Serve with whipped cream.

Preheat an oven to 425°F (220°C). Roll out the pastry and use to line a 9-inch (23-cm) pie pan. Set aside.

To make the filling, combine the pumpkin purée and pecans in the bowl of a food processor and process until smooth and well blended. Scrape the pumpkin mixture into a bowl. Beat in the eggs, then add the sugar, rum, cinnamon, ginger and cloves and blend well. Add the cream and stir until completely mixed.

Pour the pumpkin mixture into the pastry-lined pan. Bake for 10 minutes, then reduce the heat to 300°F (150°C) and bake until a knife inserted slightly off-center comes out clean, about 40 minutes longer. Serve warm or at room temperature.

Makes one 9-inch (23-cm) single-crust pie

Angel Pie

FOR THE MERINGUE CRUST:
4 egg whites
½ teaspoon cream of tartar
pinch of salt
1 cup (8 oz/250 g) sugar

FOR THE FILLING:
1 cup (8 fl oz/250 ml) heavy (double)
  cream
1 cup (11 oz/345 g) lemon curd (recipe
  on page 35), chilled

FOR THE TOPPING:
1 cup (8 fl oz/250 ml) heavy (double)
  cream
1 tablespoon sugar
1 tablespoon nonfat dry milk (milk
  powder)
8–10 whole strawberries or ½ cup
  (2 oz/60 g) raspberries (optional)

Traditionally angel pie is composed of a crisp meringue shell spread with lemon custard and topped with whipped cream. Here the custard is replaced with lemon curd lightened with whipped cream, making the filling even more irresistible. The pie is usually garnished with strawberries, but raspberries or sliced peaches will also complement the filling. If fresh fruit is out of season, decorate the pie with candied ginger or violets, or even shaved chocolate.

*P*reheat an oven to 275°F (135°C). Generously butter a 9-inch (23-cm) glass pie dish. To make the crust, in a medium-sized bowl, combine the egg whites, cream of tartar and salt. Beat until the egg whites stand in soft peaks. Slowly add the sugar, continuing to beat until stiff peaks form. Spread the egg whites over the bottom and sides of the prepared pie dish, making the edges about 1 inch (2.5 cm) thick and building them slightly above the rim of the dish. Bake until golden brown and firm, about 1¼ hours. Turn off the oven and let the crust cool completely in the oven with the door ajar; overnight is okay.

To make the filling, whip the cream until stiff peaks form, then gently fold in the lemon curd. Spread the mixture in the meringue shell.

To make the topping, combine the cream, sugar and dry milk in a bowl. Whip until stiff and spread over the pie. Garnish with berries, if desired.

Makes one 9-inch (23-cm) pie

Peanut Butter Chiffon Pie

crumb crust for a 9-inch (23-cm) pie
shell, made with graham crackers or
chocolate wafers *(recipe on page 14)*
1 envelope (1 tablespoon) unflavored
gelatin
¼ cup (2 fl oz/60 ml) water
4 eggs, separated
1 cup (8 oz/250 g) sugar
1 cup (8 oz/250 g) smooth peanut butter
1 cup (8 fl oz/250 ml) milk
½ cup (4 fl oz/125 ml) heavy (double)
cream
¼ cup (1 oz/30 g) chopped toasted
peanuts (optional)

Chiffon fillings are airy and delicate, with a framework supported by unflavored gelatin. The taste of this pie appeals especially to children, but any peanut butter enthusiast will be satisfied. Top each slice with a spoonful of whipped cream.

Preheat an oven to 325°F (180°C). Pat the crumb mixture into a 9-inch (23-cm) pie pan and bake for 8 minutes. Remove from the oven and let cool completely before filling.

In a small bowl sprinkle the gelatin over the water and let stand for a few minutes to soften. Meanwhile, put the egg yolks in a medium saucepan and whisk them for a moment. Stir in ¾ cup (6 oz/190 g) of the sugar, the peanut butter and milk. Place over medium heat and cook, stirring constantly, until the mixture just reaches a simmer and thickens slightly but does not boil. Remove from the heat and add the softened gelatin, stirring until it is completely dissolved. Pour into a bowl and refrigerate, stirring now and then, until it mounds slightly when dropped from a spoon and no longer feels warm, about 1 hour or more.

Whip the cream until stiff. In another bowl beat the egg whites until soft peaks form. Slowly add the remaining ¼ cup (2 oz/60 g) sugar to the whites, continuing to beat until stiff peaks form. Gently fold the beaten egg whites and cream into the peanut butter mixture until completely blended. Mound the mixture in the crust and sprinkle with the peanuts, if desired. Chill several hours before serving.

Makes one 9-inch (23-cm) single-crust pie

Sugar Tart

tart pastry for a 9-inch (23-cm) tart shell
  (recipe on page 13)
3 eggs
¾ cup (6 oz/185 g) sugar
2 tablespoons cornmeal
1 tablespoon cider vinegar
¼ teaspoon salt
7 tablespoons (3½ oz/110 g) unsalted
  butter, melted

FOR THE TOPPING:
⅓ cup (3 oz/90 g) sugar
1 tablespoon unsalted butter, chilled
½ teaspoon ground cinnamon or
  nutmeg

*A delicate tart that tastes of butter, sugar and cream.
The spicy, crunchy topping is a good contrast to the smooth
custard underneath.*

Preheat an oven to 425°F (220°C). Roll out the pastry and
use to line a 9-inch (23-cm) tart pan. Bake the crust fully,
until browned and crisp (see page 10 for detailed instructions). Cool completely before filling. Reduce the oven
temperature to 325°F (165°C).

In a mixing bowl combine the eggs, sugar, cornmeal,
vinegar, salt and butter. Beat until smooth. Pour the egg
mixture into the tart shell. Bake until the custard is barely
set and the center still quivers, about 30 minutes.

Meanwhile, make the topping. In a small bowl combine
the sugar, butter and cinnamon or nutmeg. With your
fingertips rapidly work the ingredients together until
blended; the mixture should be light and dry. When the tart
has baked for 30 minutes and is barely set, carefully remove
it from the oven and sprinkle it with the topping. Return the
tart to the oven and bake until the filling is set and the
topping has melted a little, about 10 minutes longer.

Makes one 9-inch (23-cm) tart

Chocolate-Rum Chiffon Pie

crumb crust for a 9-inch (23-cm) pie
   shell, made with graham crackers or
   chocolate wafers (recipe on page 14)
1 envelope (1 tablespoon) unflavored
   gelatin
1 cup (8 fl oz/250 ml) brewed coffee, at
   room temperature
½ cup (4 fl oz/125 ml) milk
2 oz (60 g) unsweetened (cooking)
   chocolate, chopped
½ cup (4 oz/125 g) sugar
¼ teaspoon salt
3 eggs, separated
2 tablespoons rum
1 teaspoon vanilla extract (essence)
1 cup (8 fl oz/250 ml) heavy (double)
   cream

*The flavors of chocolate and rum are especially satisfying
after a rich meal. If you wish, you can make this pie without
the crust by simply mounding the filling in an oiled pie plate
and serving it with some sugar cookies or shortbread.*

Preheat an oven to 325°F (180°C). Press the crumb
mixture into a 9-inch (23-cm) pie pan and bake for 8
minutes. Cool completely before filling.

   Sprinkle the gelatin over the coffee and let stand for a few
minutes. Meanwhile, in a saucepan, combine the milk and
chocolate. Place over low heat and cook, stirring constantly,
until the chocolate melts. Remove from the heat, add ¼ cup
(2 oz/60 g) of the sugar, the salt and egg yolks and whisk
until blended. Return to moderate heat and cook, stirring
constantly, until the mixture thickens slightly and barely
reaches a simmer, about 5 minutes; do not allow it to boil.

   Add the softened gelatin and stir over the heat about
1 minute longer. Pour the chocolate mixture into a bowl
and refrigerate, stirring occasionally, until it mounds when
dropped from a spoon and is the consistency of unbeaten
egg whites, about 1 hour. Stir in the rum and vanilla.

   Whip the cream until stiff. In another bowl and with
clean beaters, beat the egg whites until soft peaks form.
Slowly add the remaining ¼ cup (2 oz/65 g) sugar, continuing to beat until stiff peaks form. Fold the cream and
egg whites into the chocolate mixture and pile into the pie
shell. Chill several hours before serving.

Makes one 9-inch (23-cm) single-crust pie

Macadamia-Coconut Tart

tart pastry for a 9-inch (23-cm) tart shell
   (recipe on page 13)
½ cup (4 oz/125 g) unsalted butter
¾ cup (6 oz/185 g) sugar
½ cup (4 fl oz/125 ml) heavy (double)
   cream
2 teaspoons freshly grated lemon zest
1 cup (3 oz/90 g) macadamia nuts,
   coarsely chopped
½ cup (1½ oz/45 g) packaged grated
   coconut, lightly toasted
3 tablespoons bourbon or rum
1 teaspoon vanilla extract (essence)

A fancy-looking tart that is ideal for special occasions and isn't difficult to make. The filling becomes golden brown and caramelizes in the oven. If your macadamias are salted, rinse them and spread them out to dry on paper towels before chopping.

❧

Preheat an oven to 425°F (220°C). Roll out the pastry and use to line a 9-inch (23-cm) tart pan. Bake the crust partially, until the pastry looks dry but is still very pale (see page 10 for detailed instructions). Cool completely before filling. Reduce the oven temperature to 350°F (180°C).

In a medium saucepan over moderate heat, melt the butter. Add the sugar and bring to a boil; boil for 2 minutes, stirring constantly. Remove from the heat and stir in the cream, lemon zest, macadamia nuts and coconut. Bring the mixture back to a boil, then remove from the heat and stir in the bourbon (or rum) and vanilla.

Pour the mixture into the cooled tart shell. Bake until the filling is bubbly and thick and the tart is golden brown, about 30 minutes. Cool for about 5 minutes.

Remove the tart from the pan while it is still warm; it can be difficult to remove when it is cold.

Makes one 9-inch (23-cm) tart

Black-and-White Fudge Pie

chocolate-walnut pastry for a 9-inch
   (23-cm) pie shell (*recipe on page 16*)

FOR THE CHOCOLATE BATTER:
½ cup (4 oz/125 g) unsalted butter
4 oz (125 g) bittersweet (plain)
   chocolate, broken into pieces
2 eggs
⅔ cup (5 oz/155 g) sugar
¼ cup (1 oz/30g) all-purpose (plain) flour
¼ teaspoon salt
½ cup (1 oz/30 g) chopped walnuts

FOR THE CREAM CHEESE MIXTURE:
8 oz (250 g) cream cheese, at room
   temperature
⅓ cup (3 oz/90 g) sugar
1 egg
1 teaspoon vanilla extract (essence)

This pie looks like a contest winner, with cream cheese swirled into a brownie-type batter and baked in a chocolate crust. It is inspired by the black and white brownies made by pastry chef Emily Luchetti at Stars in San Francisco.

Preheat an oven to 425°F (220°C). Press the pastry into a 9-inch (23-cm) pie pan (or roll it out after chilling the dough for 1 hour). Bake the crust partially (see page 10 for detailed instructions). Cool completely before filling. Reduce the oven temperature to 325°F (180°C).

To make the chocolate batter, in a double boiler over simmering water, stir the chocolate and butter together until melted and smooth, about 5 minutes; set aside. In a mixing bowl beat the eggs until blended. Add the sugar, flour and salt and beat until well mixed. Stir in the melted chocolate and walnuts. Remove ½ cup (4 fl oz/125 ml) of the batter and set aside; spread the remainder in the cooled pie shell.

To make the cream cheese mixture, in another bowl beat the cream cheese until smooth. Beat in the sugar, egg and vanilla until well blended. Spread the cheese mixture over the chocolate batter in the pie shell—do not worry about getting it perfectly even—then spoon the reserved chocolate batter randomly over the top. With a knife, swirl the batters together to form a marbled effect.

Bake until the filling is set, about 40 minutes. Serve at room temperature or chilled.

Makes one 9-inch (23-cm) single-crust pie

Lemon Tart

rich tart pastry for a 9-inch (23-cm) tart shell *(recipe on page 14)*

6 lemons

2 cups (1 lb/500 g) sugar

½ cup (4 fl oz/125 ml) water

2 eggs

½ cup (4 fl oz/125 ml) heavy (double) cream

pinch of salt

½ cup (5 oz/155 g) apricot jam

An unusual tart because it uses whole lemon slices, simmered in sugar syrup then arranged on a delicate lemon custard.

Preheat an oven to 425°F (220°C). Line a 9-inch (23-cm) tart pan with the pastry. Bake fully until browned and crisp (see page 10 for detailed instructions). Cool completely.

Grate the zest from 2 lemons and juice them; you need about ⅓ cup (3 fl oz/80 ml) juice. Set aside. With a knife, peel the remaining 4 lemons, cutting deeply enough to remove all the white pith and expose the flesh all around. Slice crosswise ¼ inch (6 mm) thick. Pick out any seeds.

Combine 1½ cups (12 oz/375 g) of the sugar with the water in a saucepan. Stir over low heat until the sugar dissolves, then increase the heat and boil to the soft-ball stage, 238°F (115°C). Add the lemon slices and bring back to a simmer. Remove from the heat; set aside for at least 1 hour.

Preheat an oven to 350°F (180°C). Beat together the reserved lemon juice and lemon zest, the remaining ½ cup (4 oz/125 g) sugar and the eggs. Stir in the cream and salt. Pour into the cooled tart shell and bake until just set, about 20 minutes. Cool to room temperature.

Carefully lift the lemon slices from the syrup and lay them on the filling—two forks are useful for this. In a small saucepan combine ¼ cup (2 fl oz/60 ml) of the cooking syrup with the apricot jam and boil for several minutes, until thick. Strain to remove the pulp. Brush the glaze over the lemon slices. Serve as soon as possible.

Makes one 9-inch (23-cm) tart

Ginger-Carrot Pie

basic pie pastry for a 9-inch (23-cm) pie
   shell (*recipe on page 12*)
1½ cups (12 oz/375 g) unseasoned,
   puréed cooked carrot
3 eggs
⅓ cup (3 oz/90 g) sugar
⅓ cup (4 oz/125 g) honey
freshly grated zest of 1 orange
2 tablespoons chopped candied ginger
1 teaspoon ground nutmeg
½ teaspoon ground cinnamon
¼ teaspoon ground allspice
½ teaspoon salt
1 cup (8 fl oz/250 ml) heavy (double)
   cream

*Even if you dislike the vegetable, you'll enjoy the pie.
It's spicy and sweet, and although the carrot flavor is subtle,
it is definitely there. Cooked, mashed parsnips work equally
well in a pie.*

❧

Preheat an oven to 425°F (220°C). Roll out the pastry and
use to line a 9-inch (23-cm) pie pan. Set aside.

   In a large mixing bowl, combine the carrot, eggs, sugar,
honey, orange zest, ginger, nutmeg, cinnamon, allspice and
salt. Beat until smooth. Stir in the cream and beat until well
blended. Pour the carrrot mixture into the pastry-lined pan.

   Bake for 15 minutes, then reduce the heat to 300°F
(150°C) and bake until the filling is set around the edges
and a knife inserted slightly off-center comes out clean,
30–40 minutes longer. Serve warm or at room temperature.

Makes one 9-inch (23-cm) single-crust pie

Black Bottom Tart

tart pastry for a 9-inch (23-cm) tart shell
  (*recipe on page 13*)
2 teaspoons unflavored gelatin
¼ cup (2 fl oz/60 ml) water
1¼ cups (10 fl oz/310 ml) milk
2 eggs, separated
½ cup (4 oz/125 g) sugar
1 tablespoon cornstarch (cornflour)
¼ teaspoon salt
1 oz (30 g) unsweetened (cooking)
  chocolate, melted
1 teaspoon vanilla extract (essence)
¼ cup (2 fl oz/60 ml) dark rum

FOR THE TOPPING:
½ cup (4 fl oz/125 ml) heavy (double)
  cream
2 teaspoons sugar
1 tablespoon grated unsweetened
  (cooking) chocolate

A layer of chocolate crowned with an airy rum chiffon.

Preheat an oven to 425°F (220°C). Roll out the pastry and use to line a 9-inch (23-cm) tart pan. Bake the crust fully, until browned and crisp (see page 10 for detailed instructions). Cool completely before filling.

Sprinkle the gelatin over the water and let stand for a few minutes. Bring the milk to a simmer in a saucepan. Slowly pour the hot milk over the egg yolks, whisking constantly. Pour the mixture back into the saucepan off the heat.

Stir together ⅓ cup (3 oz/90 g) of the sugar, the cornstarch and salt. Add to the milk mixture along with the gelatin mixture and whisk until blended. Cook over moderate heat, stirring constantly, until the custard thickens slightly and barely reaches a simmer, about 10 minutes; do not allow it to boil. Remove from the heat. Pour ½ cup (4 fl oz/125 ml) of the custard into a small bowl and blend in the melted chocolate. Spread the chocolate mixture in the tart shell and set aside. Stir the vanilla and rum into the remaining custard and chill until it is cool and mounds when dropped from a spoon, about 1 hour.

Whip the egg whites until soft peaks form. Slowly add the remaining sugar (about 2 tablespoons), continuing to beat until stiff. Fold in the rum custard. Spread the mixture over the chocolate, mounding it slightly.

To make the topping, whip the cream and sugar until stiff, then spoon over the tart. Sprinkle with the chocolate.

Makes one 9-inch (23-cm) tart

Chocolate-Hazelnut Pie

chocolate-walnut pastry for a 9-inch
  (23-cm) pie shell (recipe on page 16)
3 tablespoons unsalted butter
2 oz (60 g) unsweetened (cooking)
  chocolate, broken into pieces
3 eggs
1 cup (8 fl oz/250 ml) light corn syrup
½ cup (4 oz/125 g) sugar
1 teaspoon vanilla extract (essence)
¼ teaspoon salt
1½ cups (6 oz/185 g) coarsely chopped,
  peeled and lightly toasted hazelnuts
  (filberts)

This is no ordinary hazelnut pie. There is a double dose of chocolate—it's in the pastry and the filling—and the texture is moist and brownielike. This combination will appeal to anyone with a sweet tooth. Serve it with vanilla ice cream or unsweetened whipped cream.

Preheat an oven to 425°F (220°C). Press the pastry into a 9-inch (23-cm) pie pan (or roll it out after chilling the dough for 1 hour). Set it aside.

   Combine the butter and chocolate in the top pan of a double boiler placed over simmering water. Stir until melted and smooth, about 5 minutes. Remove from the heat and set aside.

   In a mixing bowl beat the eggs until blended. Add the corn syrup, sugar, vanilla and salt. Beat in the chocolate mixture, then stir in the hazelnuts.

   Pour the mixture into the pastry-lined pan. Bake for 20 minutes, then reduce the heat to 350°F (180°C) and bake until the filling is set around the edges and the center quivers slightly, about 25 minutes longer.

Makes one 9-inch (23-cm) single-crust pie

Banbury Tart

tart pastry for a 9-inch (23-cm) tart shell
  (recipe on page 13)
1½ cups (8 oz/250 g) raisins
1 cup (8 fl oz/250 ml) water
⅔ cup (5 oz/155 g) sugar
4 soda crackers, finely crushed
2 teaspoons freshly grated lemon zest
2 tablespoons fresh lemon juice
1 egg, beaten

FOR THE TOPPING:
½ cup (3 oz/90 g) all-purpose (plain)
  flour
3 tablespoons unsalted butter
2 tablespoons sugar
¼ teaspoon salt

A full-sized version of the individual raisin tarts from Banbury, England. This has a streusel topping, and the dark filling looks and tastes remarkably like mincemeat.

Preheat an oven to 400°F (200°C). Roll out the pastry and use to line a 9-inch (23-cm) tart pan. Bake partially, until the pastry looks dry but is still very pale (see page 10 for detailed instructions). Cool completely before filling.

In a heavy-bottomed saucepan, combine the raisins, water, sugar, crackers and lemon zest. Bring to a boil over high heat. Reduce the heat to low and simmer until slightly thickened, about 10 minutes. Remove from the heat and stir in the lemon juice and egg; set aside.

To make the topping, combine the flour, butter, sugar and salt in a small bowl. With your fingertips, blend together the ingredients until the mixture resembles fine crumbs.

Pour the raisin mixture into the cooled tart shell and sprinkle the crumb mixture evenly over the top. Bake until lightly browned on top, about 35 minutes.

Makes one 9-inch (23-cm) tart

Sweet Potato Soufflé Pie

basic pie pastry for a 9-inch (23-cm) pie
   shell *(recipe on page 12)*
1½ cups (12 oz/375 g) mashed, cooked
   sweet potatoes
¾ cup (4 oz/125 g) firmly packed brown
   sugar
3 eggs, separated
1 teaspoon ground cinnamon
1 teaspoon ground ginger
½ teaspoon ground mace
¼ teaspoon salt
1½ cups (12 fl oz/375 ml), or more, milk
   or heavy (double) cream
2 tablespoons sugar

*Sweet potatoes and yams may be used interchangeably in
this pie, although yams are darker and sweeter. The filling
has a texture that is slightly coarse but not dry, and the
beaten egg whites give it lightness. The amount of filling is
generous, so be sure to have a high fluted crust.*

*P*reheat an oven to 425°F (220°C). Roll out the pastry and
use to line a 9-inch (23-cm) pie pan. Set aside.

In a large bowl combine the sweet potatoes, brown sugar,
egg yolks, cinnamon, ginger, mace and salt. Beat until
smooth. Stir in 1½ cups (12 fl oz/375 ml) milk or cream.
The mixture should have the consistency of hot cereal;
if it is too thick, it will be difficult to fold in the egg whites.
If necessary add a little more milk or cream to achieve the
correct consistency.

In another bowl beat the egg whites until soft peaks form.
Slowly add the white sugar, continuing to beat until stiff
peaks form. Stir a heaping spoonful of the whites into the
sweet potato mixture to lighten it, then fold in the
remaining whites.

Pour the sweet potato mixture into the pastry-lined pan.
Bake for 15 minutes, then reduce the heat to 300°F (150°C)
and bake until the filling is set and a knife inserted slightly
off-center comes out clean, about 65 minutes longer. Turn
off the heat, set the oven door ajar and let the pie cool for 20
minutes, then remove it from the oven. Serve warm or at
room temperature.

Makes one 9-inch (23-cm) single-crust pie

Lime Chiffon Pie

crumb crust for a 9-inch (23-cm) pie
 shell, made with graham crackers
 (recipe on page 14)
1 envelope (1 tablespoon) unflavored
 gelatin
⅓ cup (3 fl oz/80 ml) water
1 cup (8 oz/250 g) sugar
⅔ cup (5 fl oz/160 ml) fresh lime juice
5 eggs, separated
1 tablespoon freshly grated lime zest
2 tablespoons tequila (optional)

*Before electric mixers were standard equipment, anything
with beaten egg whites required patience and effort. Here is
an adaptation of the "mile-high pies" that were popular
decades ago, when electric beaters were coming on the
market to relieve cooks of the "elbow grease" needed to whip
egg whites. The filling may also be made with lemon juice,
and as the name implies, it is light and lofty.*

Preheat an oven to 325°F (180°C). Press the crumb
mixture into a 9-inch (23-cm) pie pan and bake for 8
minutes. Cool completely before filling.

In a heavy-bottomed saucepan, sprinkle the gelatin over
the water and let stand for a few minutes to soften. Add
½ cup (4 oz/125 g) of the sugar and the lime juice and mix
well. Then add the egg yolks and whisk until blended.
Place over moderate heat and cook, stirring constantly, until
the mixture thickens slightly and barely reaches a simmer,
5–10 minutes; do not allow it to boil. Stir in the lime zest.
Pour the gelatin mixture into a bowl and refrigerate, stirring
occasionally, until it mounds when dropped from a spoon
and is the consistency of unbeaten egg whites, about 1 hour.
Stir in the tequila, if desired.

In a medium bowl beat the egg whites until soft peaks
form, then gradually add the remaining ½ cup (4 oz/125 g)
sugar and beat until stiff peaks form. Gently fold the lime
mixture into the whites, then pile it into the crust. Chill
several hours before serving.

Makes one 9-inch (23-cm) single-crust pie

Maple-Pecan Pie

tart pastry for a 9-inch (23-cm) tart shell
  (recipe on page 13)
3 eggs
1 cup (8 fl oz/250 ml) maple syrup
¼ cup (2 fl oz/60 ml) dark corn syrup
¼ cup (2 oz/60 g) sugar
¼ cup (2 oz/60 g) unsalted butter,
  melted
1 teaspoon vanilla extract (essence)
¼ teaspoon salt
1½ cups (5 oz/155 g) pecan halves

Here is a pie that is excellent for cutting into small wedges and serving with afternoon coffee or tea. Accompany it with unsweetened whipped cream, if you wish. Pecans are a perfect foil for the subtle taste of maple syrup, and although a simple pie pastry will work, the buttery flavor of tart pastry is especially good with this filling.

Preheat an oven to 425°F (220°C). Roll out the pastry and use to line a 9-inch (23-cm) pie pan. Set it aside.

In a large bowl beat the eggs until blended. Add the maple syrup, corn syrup, sugar, butter, vanilla and salt; beat until thoroughly combined. Stir in the pecan halves.

Pour the pecan mixture into the pastry-lined pan. Bake for 15 minutes, then reduce the heat to 350°F (180°C) and bake until the filling has puffed and set around the edges but the center is slightly soft, about 25 minutes longer. Serve warm or at room temperature.

Makes one 9-inch (23-cm) single-crust pie

Glossary

The following glossary defines terms specifically as they relate to pies and tarts. Included are major and unusual ingredients, essential equipment and basic techniques.

ALLSPICE
Sweet spice of Caribbean origin with a flavor suggesting a blend of cinnamon, cloves and nutmeg, hence its name. May be purchased as whole dried berries—resembling large dark peppercorns—or already ground.

ALUMINUM FOIL
Useful as a lining to help a pie crust keep its shape when it is partially or fully baked without a filling. Use a double-thick 12-inch (30-cm) square, punched with a few holes and pressed snugly into the bottom and sides of the crust.

BLIND BAKING
Used to describe the act of partially or fully baking a pie crust before filling.

BUTTER
For pie-making purposes, good-quality commercial sweet—that is, unsalted—butter is preferred but not essential.

CALVADOS
Dry French brandy distilled from apples and bearing the fruit's distinctive aroma and taste. Dry applejack may be substituted.

CANDY THERMOMETER
Thermometer specially designed to register temperatures in the 230°–350°F (110°–177°C) range to which sugar syrup–based mixtures are heated in dessert and candy making.

CARAMELIZE
To cause sugar, or the sugars present in certain fruits or other foods, to darken to a golden or brown color and develop a rich flavor through the steady application of heat.

CHOCOLATE
For pie making, purchase the best-quality baking chocolate you can find—whether unsweetened (cooking) or bittersweet or semisweet (plain) chocolate, as the recipe requires.

Cutting Chocolate Shavings
Thin shavings of chocolate make simple, pretty decorations for single-crust pies that include chocolate in their fillings.

To cut shavings, draw a vegetable peeler along the narrow edge of a chocolate block.

Melting Chocolate
Care must be taken to melt chocolate without scorching. A **double boiler,** in which the grated chocolate melts— sometimes with butter, cream,

rum or a liqueur—above water kept below a simmer, ensures gentle heat.

Fill bottom half of double boiler with water to one quarter its depth. Bring water to a boil; adjust heat to keep water below a simmer.

Add chocolate and any other ingredients to top half and place on top of bottom half, making sure top half does not touch water.

With a wooden spoon, stir chocolate continuously, until mixture is completely melted and smooth.

CARDAMOM
Sweet, exotic-tasting spice sometimes used in apple or pumpkin pies. Its small, round seeds, which come enclosed in a husklike pod, may be purchased whole or already ground.

CHIFFON
Pie filling made light and fluffy with beaten egg whites and stabilized by **gelatin.**

CINNAMON
Popular sweet spice for flavoring fruits. The aromatic bark of a type of evergreen tree, it is sold as whole dried strips—cinnamon sticks—or already ground.

CLOVES
Rich and aromatic East African spice used in its ground form in pie making, or whole in poached-fruit syrups.

COCONUT
Although packaged dried coconut may be used in pie making, the flavor of fresh coconut is superior. Choose a ripe coconut in which liquid can be heard when the fruit is shaken.

With a sharp, sturdy skewer, carefully pierce the three round, fleshy depressions found at one end. Drain out the liquid. With a cleaver, carefully crack the coconut open near the end opposite the holes. Using a small, sharp, sturdy knife, carefully pry the white flesh from the shell (if this proves difficult, dry the coconut pieces in a 350°F (180°C) oven for 15–20 minutes). Peel the brown skin from the flesh. Coarsely grate the flesh with a hand grater or food processor.

CORN SYRUP
Light- or dark-colored, neutral-tasting syrup extracted from corn.

CORNSTARCH (CORNFLOUR)
Fine, powdery flour ground from the endosperm of corn—the white heart of the kernel—and used as a

neutral-flavored thickening agent in some pie fillings.

CREAM OF TARTAR

Acidic powder extracted during wine making that is used in pie making as an additive to **meringue,** serving both to stabilize the egg whites and to increase their heat tolerance. Also used as a leavening agent, most commonly combined with baking soda to make commercial baking powder, and as an ingredient in sugar syrups to prevent crystallization.

CRÈME FRAÎCHE

French-style lightly soured and thickened fresh cream, sometimes used as a topping or garnish for fruit pies. Increasingly available in supermarkets, although a similar product may be prepared at home by stirring 2 teaspoons well-drained sour cream into 1 cup (8 fl oz/250 ml) lightly whipped heavy (double) cream. Or, to make your own crème fraîche, stir 1 teaspoon cultured buttermilk into 1 cup (8 fl oz/250 ml) heavy (double) cream. Cover tightly and leave at warm room temperature until thickened, about 12 hours. Refrigerate until ready to serve. Will keep for up to 1 week.

CRISP

Pie or other fruit dessert baked with a sweet, crumblike topping—usually featuring rolled oats—that crisps up in the oven.

CRUMBLE

Pie or other fruit dessert topped with a fine streusel mixture that bakes to a crisp, crumbly consistency in the oven.

CRUST, CRUMB

Single pie crust made from a mixture of crushed graham crackers or cookies, sugar, salt

and butter and pressed by hand into the pan. Often used for rich or thick fillings such as cheese, cream or **chiffon** mixtures.

CRUST, DOUBLE

Refers to a pie made with both a bottom and a top crust.

CRUST, SINGLE

Refers to a pie made with only a bottom crust.

CURD

Thick, custardlike pie or tart filling flavored with juice and **zest** of citrus fruit, usually lemon, although lime and orange may also be used.

CUSTARD

Thick, rich, sweet mixture—popular as a pie filling—made by gently cooking together egg yolks, sugar, milk or cream, and sometimes other flavorings.

DEEP DISH

Refers to a fruit pie baked in a dish at least 2 inches (5 cm) deep, and usually with only a top crust.

DOUBLE BOILER

Stove-top device designed for cooking over very low heat. The bottom part of the double boiler holds water, which is brought to a boil on the stove and then held at low heat, usually a bare simmer or less. The slightly smaller top portion of the double boiler fits inside the lower pan, allowing cooking over the gentle heat of the water.

   To improvise a double boiler, fill a medium- to large-sized saucepan with water to about one quarter of its depth. Boil the water and adjust the heat as required by the recipe. Set a smaller saucepan, or a heatproof metal or glass bowl, on top, so that its bottom rests above the hot water.

DOUGH SCRAPER

Kitchen tool consisting of a sturdy, rectangular metal blade with a handle along one side, used to lift dough and scrape the work surface clean.

EGGS

Separating Eggs

Many pie recipes call for separating egg yolks and whites. To separate an egg, crack the shell in half by tapping it against the side of a bowl and then breaking it apart with your fingers. Holding the shell halves over the bowl, gently transfer the whole yolk back and forth between them, letting the clear white drop away into the bowl and taking care not to cut into the yolk with the edges of the shell. Transfer the yolk to another bowl.

   Alternatively, gently pour the egg from the shell onto the slightly cupped fingers of your outstretched hand, held over a bowl. Let the whites fall between your fingers into the bowl; the whole yolk will remain in your hand. The same basic function is also performed by an aluminum, ceramic or plastic egg separator, which holds the yolk intact in its cuplike center while allowing the white to drip out through one or more slots in its side, into a bowl placed below.

Whisking Eggs

Through a harmless chemical reaction, an unlined half-sphere copper bowl strengthens egg whites during beating,

FLOUR, ALL-PURPOSE (PLAIN)

No special variety of flour is necessary for making pie pastry—just the all-purpose, bleached, blended (hard and soft wheats) flour available in all supermarkets.

allowing them to achieve a greater, more stable volume. If you don't have a copper bowl, a little **cream of tartar** added to the whites will also stabilize them, although it will not increase their volume.

   Put the whites into a large bowl. With a wire balloon whisk, or an electric beater at medium speed, beat the whites with broad, sweeping strokes to incorporate as much air as possible. As the whites begin to thicken and turn a glossy, snowy white, lift out the whisk or beater: If a soft peak forms, then droops back on itself, the whites have reached the "soft peak" stage.

For "stiff peak" whites, continue beating until the whites form stiff, unmoving peaks when the whisk or beater is lifted out.

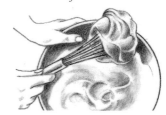

FLUTE

To seal the dough along the rim of a double-crust pie, or to decorate the rim of a single-crust pie. Any number of methods may be used; here are just a few.

Hold the thumb and forefinger of one hand outside the rim. With your other thumb, push the dough to form a pleat. Repeat at close intervals to form an evenly pleated rim.

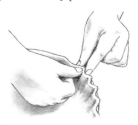

Or, with a thumb on top of the rim and a forefinger underneath, pinch together the dough edges, pressing the thumb down into the dough. Repeat at close intervals all around the rim.

Alternatively, press the tines of a table fork down into the pastry, just deep enough to make a distinct impression. Continue all around the rim.

FOLDING

To blend together two mixtures of different consistencies—most often folding beaten egg whites or whipped cream into a thicker mixture. To fold in the whites without deflating them, first use a rubber spatula to stir a generous dollop of the whites gently into the other mixture, lightening it. Then add the remaining whites, gently lifting and turning the two mixtures up and down in a folding motion until blended. Be careful not to overmix or the mixture will lose its lightness.

FREE-FORM TART

Tart formed on a baking sheet without use of a **tart ring**, taking any shape that the cook wishes. An approach most commonly used for fresh fruit tarts.

GELATIN

Unflavored commercial gelatin gives delicate body to **chiffon** fillings. Sold in ¼-ounce (about 1-tablespoon) envelopes, each of which is sufficient to set about 2 cups (16 fl oz/500 ml) liquid.

GINGER

The root of the tropical ginger plant, which yields a sweet, strong-flavored spice. The whole root may be purchased fresh in a supermarket fruit and vegetable section. Pieces of root may be found crystallized or candied in the supermarket baking department, or preserved in syrup in the Asian food section. Dried and ground ginger is commonly available in jars or tins in the spice section.

GLAZE

Light, sweet coating—usually made from fruit jelly—applied as an attractively glistening and flavorful finish to fruit tarts. May also be brushed inside a fully baked tart shell before a filling is added, to seal the bottom crust and keep it crisp.

KIRSCH

Dry, clear brandy distilled from black morello cherries and infused with their unique aroma and taste. Do not confuse with crème de kirsch, a sweet cherry liqueur.

LATTICE TOP

Decorative, basketlike weaving of pie dough strips on top of a filling, usually fruit.

MANGO

Tropical fruit with a very juicy, aromatic orange flesh. Ripe mangoes yield slightly to finger pressure; ripen firm mangoes at room temperature in an open paper or plastic bag. Slit with a knife, the skin peels easily. Slice the flesh from both sides of the large, flat pit, as well as from around its edges.

MAPLE SYRUP

Syrup derived from the sap of the maple tree, with an inimitably rich savor and intense sweetness. Buy maple syrup labeled "pure," rather than a blend.

MERINGUE

Topping of sweetened, beaten egg whites, browned under a broiler (griller). Meringue may also be used to line a tart pan or pie pan, then baked to form a crisp shell for fruit or custard fillings.

MINCEMEAT

Old-fashioned pie or tart filling made from raisins and dried currants, apples, candied citron, sweeteners and spices. Originally, it also included finely ground beef and suet.

NUTMEG

Popular baking spice that is the hard pit of the fruit of the nutmeg tree. May be bought already ground; or preferably whole, to be freshly ground as needed with any fine grater or a special nutmeg grater or grinder.

PAPAYA

Tropical fruit shaped somewhat like a large pear or avocado, with soft, sweet orange flesh—milder tasting than a **mango**—and smooth yellow skin. When ripe, a papaya yields gently to finger pressure; ripen green papayas in a bowl at room temperature. Halve lengthwise and scoop out the shiny black seeds before peeling.

PARTIALLY BAKED

Used to describe a pie or tart shell that has been baked briefly before a partially cooked filling is added, so that, after further baking, both pastry and filling are done simultaneously.

PASTRY BLENDER

Kitchen tool made of several parallel bands of sturdy wire, used for cutting butter or **shortening** into flour when making pastry dough by hand.

PASTRY CREAM

Thick, creamy custard used as a tart filling, often as a base for fresh fruit toppings.

PERSIMMON

An autumn fruit with a smooth, almost jellylike reddish-orange flesh and a mild, sweet, aromatic flavor. Use the Hachiya (American) variety, slightly tapered in shape and extremely soft when ripe, rather than the hard and flatter Fuyu (Asian) variety.

PIE PAN

Shallow baking pan for pies, made of metal or heatproof glass or porcelain, with smooth, sloping sides and a horizontal rim. Standard pie pans measure 9 inches (23 cm) in diameter, within the rim.

PIE WEIGHTS

Small, bean-shaped metal pellets traditionally used to fill a bottom pie crust—and thereby help it keep its shape—while it is **partially baked** or fully baked without a filling. Crust should be lined with waxed or parchment paper before weights are added, to facilitate their removal. Dried beans or peas may be used in place of metal weights. A double layer of heavy **aluminum foil,** punched with holes and pressed down into the crust before baking, serves the same purpose as the weights.

PIPING

Using a pastry bag to shape and apply a decorative topping, usually **meringue** or whipped cream. Select a pastry bag with a good-sized plain or star-shaped metal pastry tip (one designated No. 6 size or larger will be fine for most pie-decorating needs).

Drop the tip into the bag so it protrudes from the narrow opening, then twist the tip and bag to close while filling. Spoon the mixture to be piped into the bag, filling it only half full, then hold the top of the bag by its edges and shake it over a bowl or the sink to eliminate air pockets. Twist the bag shut and squeeze gently but firmly to pipe.

QUINCE

Yellowish green fruit, resembling a lumpy pear, with hard flesh that tastes harshly acidic when raw. Cooked in sugar syrup, the fruit develops a delicate, sweet flavor.

RHUBARB

Perennial plant whose stems resemble large, salmon-colored celery stalks. Although a vegetable, rhubarb is most commonly eaten as a fruit, cooked and sweetened with sugar and often combined with strawberries or raspberries. Avoid the leaves and roots, which can be toxic.

ROLLING PIN

Important tool for rolling out pastry dough. Choose a hardwood rolling pin at least 12 inches (30 cm) long, to enable you to roll out dough wide enough to line a pie or tart pan. Solid dowel-type pins offer best control. Avoid water-filled glass pins, which can sweat and make pie dough sticky.

SHELL

Bottom crust of a pie, or a tart crust.

SHORTENING

Solid vegetable fat (vegetable lard) sometimes used in place of or in combination with butter in pie or tart dough. The fat is said to "shorten" the flour, that is, make it flaky or tender.

SOFT-BALL STAGE

Describes sugar syrup boiled until a spoonful dropped in ice water can be formed into a very soft, sticky ball. Equivalent to 234°–240°F (112°–116°C) on a candy thermometer.

TAPIOCA, QUICK-COOKING

Ground flakes of the tropical manioc plant's dried, starchy root. Used as a thickener for fillings.

TART

One-crust relative of the pie, baked in a vertical-sided pan or **free-form** on a baking sheet.

TART PAN

Metal, straight-sided pan—generally 9 inches (23 cm) in diameter—in which a tart is baked. Those with removable bottoms are best, allowing the tart to be unmolded before serving. Tart pans have no rims, and may have either smooth or fluted sides.

TART RING

Bottomless metal ring—which may be circular, rectangular or some other shape—used on a baking sheet to form tarts.

VANILLA

Dried aromatic pod of a variety of orchid; one of the most popular flavorings in dessert making. Most commonly used as an alcohol-based extract (essence); be sure to purchase products labeled "pure vanilla extract."

VENTS

Small slits cut in the top crust of a pie to allow steam to escape during baking.

ZEST

Thin, brightly colored, outermost layer of a citrus fruit's peel, containing most of its aromatic essential oils—a rich source of flavor for pie fillings. Zest may be removed using one of two easy methods:

1. Use a simple tool known as a zester, drawing its sharp-edged holes across the fruit's skin to remove the zest in thin strips. Alternatively, use a fine hand-held grater.

2. Holding the edge of a paring knife or vegetable peeler away from you and almost parallel to the fruit's skin, carefully cut off the zest in thin strips, taking care not to remove any white pith with it.

Then thinly slice or chop on a cutting board.

Index

ACKNOWLEDGMENTS

The publishers would like to thank the following people and organizations for
their generous assistance and support in producing this book:
Margaret D. Fallon,
Janique Poncelet, Ruth Jacobson,
Jane Fraser, Amy Morton,
Ken DellaPenta, Rapid Lasergraphics (San Francisco),
Laura Jerrard, Susan Massey-Weil, Danielle di Salvo,
Maria Antonis, Stephen Griswold, the buyers for Gardener's Eden, and the buyers and
store managers for Williams-Sonoma and Pottery Barn stores.

The following kindly lent props for the photography:
Iris Fuller, Stephanie Greenleigh, Sue Fisher King, Lorraine & Judson Puckett,
Sue White and Chuck Williams.